X
and other poems
from A to Z

X

and other poems
from A to Z

Worth Bateman

Trafford
PUBLISHING

Bloomington, Indiana

Order this book online at www.trafford.com
or email orders@trafford.com

Most Trafford titles are also available at major online book retailers.

Printed in the United States of America.

ISBN: 978-1-4669-2618-9 (sc)
ISBN: 978-1-4669-2620-2 (hc)
ISBN: 978-1-4669-2619-6 (e)

Library of Congress Control Number: 2012906084

Trafford rev. 05/10/2012

 www.trafford.com

North America & international
toll-free: 1 888 232 4444 (USA & Canada)
phone: 250 383 6864 ♦ fax: 812 355 4082

For Grace

Contents

II.

III.

Note to the Reader

The poems in this volume represent almost a decade of work in my life, work, when I began it, that seemed much different from anything I had done before. As an economist, my old work was analytical, quantitative, and often mathematical. The new work was poetry, and although I couldn't define it as well as I could define economics, from what I had read of poetry over many years, I felt sure there would be very little continuity between the old and the new.

In some ways, that has turned out to be true. On the face of it, there is little relationship between figuring out the cost of an all-volunteer armed force, designing a negative income tax, or evaluating the costs and benefits of a nuclear waste management project and writing a poem about a lemonade stand, crabcakes, or winter light. The subject matter is different as well as the know-how and the tools necessary for doing the work. Even poems about technical subjects in fields like physics or biology—and there are more here than would normally be found in a random sample of poetry books—are far from what you would find in scientific papers on the same topics.

And yet, as time has gone by, the essence of the work, old and new, as opposed to the appearance of the work, has revealed itself to be much more similar than I had originally imagined. That essence is the presence of an underlying truth which the economist or the poet is trying to describe in language. In economics, the language is frequently mathematics. It's been said "mathematics is a language," so economics could be described as the math of how markets work or the economy functions. Poetry is the math of life—the truth less narrow, the language less specialized. Looked at in this way, the fundamental nature of each endeavor is the same.

But the experience of writing poetry is not the same. Poetry is magic. Like pulling a rabbit out of a hat, it is the moment when the poetic imagination exactly captures what it was you felt, what had remained hidden from view but was there all the time, and after waiting for what often seems like so long, astounds us by its sudden appearance. For me, the joy of writing poetry is that moment.

In a body of poetic work, a whole life is revealed. It tells the story of what it is like to "locate ourselves in the thick of life," as Stanley Kunitz once described it—what it is like to be alive in one's own time and place with its conflicts and meanings, its knowns, unknowns, and unknowables. It is the story of our lives and our selves that we lay claim to, and then try to pass on.

Poetry is both digging and discovery, like archeology. And like archeology, one comes to know that the digging alone does not guarantee discovery. In the end, poetry is a gift to the poet. For me, discovery is the great pleasure of writing poetry. But I like to think poetry is not just a receiving, it is also a giving, and it is in that spirit I publish this collection of my work.

X
and other poems
from A to Z

How would the world look
if all of its things were neatly arranged
in alphabetical order? I wondered...

Billy Collins, *Nine Horses*

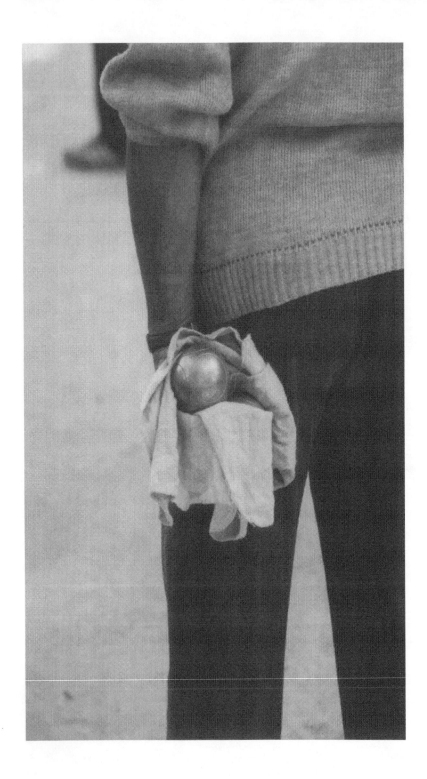

I.

Auld Lang Syne

Eight of us for dinner
to celebrate another orbit
of our aging star.
We talked of houses,
children and grandchildren,
parents and pets,
trips taken or planned,
movies worth seeing,
good places to eat.
Happily,
not much of politics
or our health.

At midnight,
we crossed the finish line
with a champagne toast to the year ahead
and then our hostess passed around
some Chinese crackers,
the kind you pull apart
to find a favor or a fortune.
Mine said, "Don't worry about avoiding temptation!
As you grow old, it starts avoiding you!"

There were also tissue paper crowns
of gold or blue which we put on
to read our fortunes.
How apropos the crowns I thought,
for us to have gotten this far,
sometimes wise,

sometimes not so wise
but still, far advanced,
still here.

Like a gathering of the crowned heads of Europe—
late eighteenth century,
before things started
turning bad.

nice comparison

My experience w/ Black snake

Blacksnake

I saw a blacksnake swallow a bird once,
a bird that hadn't learned yet to leave the nest,
a bird that couldn't fly.
There was quite a commotion up there;
I'll never forget seeing,
as if the little bird had made a headfirst dive,
the spindly legs,
quiet now,
disappearing down the all-enveloping throat.

no laughter about snake

Up there, high up,
in the stacks of the library,
in two carrels side-by-side,
was where that too began.
She was holding a large book
in her lap
and wanted me to come
look at something she had found.
I bent to see what it was,
brushed against the combed black hair,
caught the scent of her,
almost touched her neck.
She offered me a closer look
but didn't move,
so I slipped my hand
under the book,
there,
where it rested,
held it for a moment,
there,

overlooks cruelty in nature

9

before I raised it to my eyes,
which didn't dare
to look at hers.

Let's see,
where was I?
Oh yes, yes. The snake.
The first little bird was gone
so then it ate the other one.
I almost forgot
there were two of them.

Bocce Player

You don't see the game.
What you do see is a bocce player
dressed in slacks and a sweater
patiently awaiting his turn.
The photo is shot from behind;
you see part of his torso,
some of his legs,
his left arm,
and a hand,
cradling a ball in a cloth,
maybe for wiping it clean
before it is tossed.
We don't know what toss
the anonymous player will make or
once made, whether it went where he wanted;
whether it mattered,
or how many rounds he would play;
whether he won or he lost.
We don't know why he was there,
where he was from,
or where he was going
when he finished the game.
All we know is
he was there
and he played.

Caesar's Wish

We're told
when Caesar was asked how it was
he wanted to die, he answered,
Suddenly,
a wish we know he was granted,
as are we all—
the last instant of time
separating life and death
being infinitesimally small
for everyone.

I think, perhaps
what he meant to say was,
With as little warning as possible,
like a pop-quiz
rather than a final exam
or orals you'd have
plenty of time
to prepare for.

Yes, that would be better—
knowing, of course,
when the quiz was announced,
you'd never have to take another test
and it didn't matter anyway
how well it was you did.

Carousel

Flying horses
Mother called them:
three rows of stallions
gliding on invisible waves,
round and round,
ride after ride.

I remember
she had to help me up.
My feet barely reached the stirrups
when I was in the saddle,
and I was disappointed when I took the reins
at how lifeless they felt.
I didn't know about the brass ring then,
how this prize, if grasped, could be exchanged
for a treat or another ride.
All that came later.

Some mothers took the chariots
but she rode the horse next to mine,
side-saddle.
Women still wore dresses then
and that was how a lady rode.

Then it all began,
one moment at rest
the next in motion
like a train when it first begins
to leave the station.

Gently the horses climbed and fell
in a rhythm perfectly timed
to the hurdy-gurdy music.
And we went with it.

The music didn't seem to match
the fierceness of the horses' eyes,
the tension in their necks,
the outstretched legs pawing the air,
or the smoothly harnessed power
of their airborne bodies.
But nobody seemed to care.

What mattered then
was being part of this rotating universe
of movement in harmony with music,
this dance of flying horses.

Caveman

For Plato,
he could be a metaphor:
the unenlightened man,
believing only in the tangible world,
making the most he can
of a false reality,
who may emerge from the cave
but only via his mind
and the power
of pure Reason.

For me,
I'd rather picture someone
near the back of his dark cave
blinking in the gloom
after his fire has gone out,
sifting through the dead, cold ashes,
a few dry bones scattered here and there;

and the moment when he realizes
he didn't make fire itself,
that fire was something he'd been given,
had appeared long before
the ritual gathering of his few dry sticks,
was something he'd had no part in;

the moment when he knew
he'd been a fool to think
fire was something he'd created,
something he had made,

when he understood he could only do
the humble work that made
his own small fire possible,

but knowing he did have that—
even if that was all he had,
it was something—
and he believed some small good
could come from it.

Cinque Terra

We took the train from Florence here
where I wet my hands in the Ligurian Sea,
the sea where Shelley drowned
when the boat he was sailing on
went down in a storm off the coast.

Like dipping my finger
in the font of holy water
before going into church,
I wanted to make some small connection
to the man who wrote so hauntingly of death
and so passionately of life.

Somehow I'm reminded of
Dust we are and to dust
we shall return,
one of my grandmother's favorite lines.
Mopping the dust under her bed,
she liked to say someone there
was either coming or going
but wasn't sure which it was.

I think she was telling me
there is an afterlife of sorts
but one of little use to us the living,
we of the crystal waters and blue lagoons,
the pebbled beaches,
and mountains diving to the sea,
we of the towns clinging to their sides;

and me, with two small stones
now resting on a shelf
with some favorite books of poetry,
stones flat and round like well-worn coins,
picked up that day from the shore,
smoothed by the same waters
in which Shelley disappeared.

*Let us dare that ocean
that has drowned our friends*

Crabcakes

I guess it's obvious
why that meal together,
crabcakes,
eaten in the car
in a roadhouse parking lot
not long before he died,
reminds me of falling off the pier
at Riva over fifty years before
when I was ten or so
while bringing in a crab
hard pulling on a line
baited with smelt
and a hex nut for a sinker.

Uncle Bob, his older brother,
a big man with a twinkle in his eye
was standing next to me,
net in hand to dip the crab
when I got it close enough.
It's true I had leaned far out
inching Maryland's finest
to the surface just before
I went into the river,
but sure then and now
I was also helped along.

There was a moment
when I was so taken by surprise
by what had happened

I forgot to swim
and thrashed around,
helpless in the water.

Later, my father said
he was coming in for me
at just the moment I remembered
what to do,
so he didn't have to.
I hate to think how many times
since then
he must have felt the same.

Dog Bite

I was just a kid
but a kid old enough
to walk by himself
the few blocks from home
to the movie theatre downtown.
I can't remember what was playing that day,
likely a western,
maybe the Cisco Kid,
maybe the Lone Ranger and Tonto.
Leaving the house in high spirits,
about halfway there,
a dog, a dog I'd never seen before, a collie,
came racing out to the sidewalk from nowhere,
and without even a bark
or any warning whatever
sunk his teeth into the tender flesh
behind my left knee, then ran away.
The wound started to bleed
and for a moment I thought
turning back would be wise,
but the temptation of being out on my own
and going to a movie I wanted to see
was too strong
and so I went on.
The bleeding soon stopped
and when I got home,
my mother was baking a pie—
one of the many good things
mothers did then;

but by now I was starting to worry
about what could happen to me—
a bad infection or even rabies—
and I pressed her to go
to the doctor post-haste,
which she said we would do—
when the pie came out of the oven.
Surprised by this cold-hearted reply,
I asked what she thought more important:
a pie or my leg?
To which she observed:
what had waited so long for a movie
could wait a bit longer for pie.

Doing the Numbers

I'm not
sure
when I
started
doing this
or why
it all
began:
figuring
how old
my father
was
when I
was doing
such-and-such,
thinking
how
he must
have felt,
and realizing
I am
older now
than he
was then.

I do
recall
adding to
the calcu-
lations
when
he
died
how
much
time
is left
for me
if I live
as long
as he
did.

_____

Earth

What about the Gaia theory?

loves not,
cares not,
fears not,
remembers not,
withholds not,
offers not,
worries not,
regrets not,
rejoices not,
sacrifices not,
is not angered,
is not comforted,
is not proud,
is not downcast,
is not happy or sad,
does not lie down,
does not rise up,
and yet is
our mother.

Eulogy

Everything looked good on paper:
the resume of jobs and schools,
the houses he owned,
the money he'd made,
the children and grandchildren.

He'd sowed some wild oats
but his favorite movie
wasn't *Five Easy Pieces* any more.
As for Jack Nicholson,
he now preferred *Something's Gotta Give*
and he liked Paul Auster's film *Smoke*
better than either of the others.

But there was a problem.
Even on his best days
he felt like the late impatiens in the garden:
still erect after the rain,
a few nascent blooms,
but on the way out.
On other days it was worse:
more like the fall hostas:
green gone,
limp yellow leaves
drooping around the edge of the pot,
dragging on the blue stone.

Was it that "he'd been led around by his dick,
his brain turned to mush," as Erica Jong saw it;
or was it "some things just happen, that's all,"

as David Mamet thought;
or was he just "sinking under being husband and wife,"
as Robert Frost once said.

He couldn't figure it out.

Maybe it was more like notches on a gun.
You know, how cowboys
counted their killings
by cutting a knick on the handle of their Colts.
Maybe the big events in life—like the killings—
were the notches
and the spaces between each one
was all the rest.
Maybe the problem was
he hadn't cut any notches lately.

He'd had some surgery, the usual stuff,
"age appropriate," he liked to say.
He'd retired. He lived comfortably.
He loved his wife.
He'd given up drinking; done some writing.
There was the pleasant matter of the grandchildren.
But he wasn't sure if these were notches
or just part of the long space left
after the last notch he cut.

Family Farm

Gone.
Gone the spring house,
gone the mules and cows,
gone the pigs,
gone the chickens,
gone the corncrib and corn,
gone the feeding,
gone the gathering,
gone the curing and preserving,
gone the father and the mother,
gone the mother's father,
gone the mother's mother,
gone the cats that followed them to milking,
gone the barn,
gone the boy.

Still.
Still the creek,
still the frogs and minnows,
still the skippers,
still the springs,
still the water,
still the meadow,
still the hills,
still the rock outcroppings,
still the maples and the poplars,
still the oaks,
still the iris and the lilacs,
still the lilies of the valley,
still the earth.

28

Flight

A man with pruning shears in a row of vines
looks up to see a flight of geese,
their joy, like a rainbow, insisting that he look;
the earth, hundreds of feet below
under their outstretched wings.

Why all this joy?
Was it the journey?
Taking leave of winter?
Returning home?
The season of desire beginning?

"The delight of being here," he says.
Every winter now
he asked for one more year
and here he was, like the geese,
as if he too had been moved
by some sign that it was time
to begin again,
and he, like them,
had answered.

Florence via Rome

Poets seem almost useless here,
where tourists have been known
to faint from beauty,
from art laid down through centuries
like layer on geologic layer.

Even Dante could have had his doubts,
surrounded as he was by the likes of Giotto,
doubts made worse perhaps,
had he lived to see the work
of a Botticelli or a Michelangelo.

No homage to beauty has been spared here:
at the west end of this northern city,
even the Arno has been dammed just enough
to ensure a river full to its banks
and true to its bridges when the dry season comes.

Not that poets were ever any match
for an ancient coliseum,
Brunelleschi's soaring dome
or the collections of the Medici's
or Borghesi's,

busy as we are
with the light inside San Spirito,
a bunch of weathered grapes on a marble fragment,
or a manhole cover emblazoned with the letters
SPQR.

Free at Last

That year what I remember most
is not Truman beating Dewey
but picking beans in summer
for two cents a pound
in fields that seemed
to go on forever.

I could pick one hundred pounds a day;
two dollars now doesn't seem like much
but in those days
penny candy was still a penny,
a candy bar was just a nickel
and so was a Coca-Cola.

You were paid in cash at the end of each day
and the feeling going home was a good one.
I didn't know then
having money to spend as I wished
wasn't all Epictetus meant
when he said
freedom's the right to live as we please.
It's good knowing now
he was also telling us
we are free to desire the things we can't change
be exactly the way they are.

True, it's something I didn't know then,
but that was good too
while it lasted.

Ghosts

Those who say they've never seen a ghost
should have lived in the early days of television
when, long before Direct TV or cable
and before HD was even thought of,
you could often see them on the screen
with no trouble at all,
the images side-by-side
as if you were seeing double,
one image slightly offset from the other,
almost completely overlapping but not quite:

Lucy and her ghost, equally zany and appealing,
or twice the usual number of Honeymooners,
or the Poor Soul buttoning and unbuttoning
each and every button of his vest
while the Poor Soul's ghost
dutifully does the same.

You might be rid of them
if you turned the aerial just a certain way
but even when you could
it didn't last for long
and soon the same ghosts would reappear.

Like Marley's ghost in Dickens' famous tale,
I always thought the souls of the living
became the ghosts of the dead
so that calling these second images on TV
souls instead of ghosts
might have been a better choice of words.

But ghost or soul,
whatever name we choose to give the second image,
what I can't forget is how it always reappeared
regardless of our fiddling with the aerial;
as in ordinary human life
it is our authentic spirit—
what is most true about each of us,
that never really goes away for good,
and likewise in the afterlife,
whatever that may be.

Hard Sell

If we live long enough,
this we learn
from the brains of the operation
is the heart of the matter,
the bottom line, if you like,
from the head of the house:

it's not about the letter of the law,
the color of money,
knowing every trick in the book,
mastering a body of thought,
or even enjoying the luck of the Irish.

What it's all about is the art of the deal:
we can pass through the eye of the needle,
survive the perils of Pauline,
get rid of the fly in the ointment,
even escape the snake in the grass;

all we need is
the patience of Job and
the courage of our convictions.

If we stick to our knitting,
we can be the salt of the earth,
we can hear the music of the spheres;
all it takes is a labor of love.

Iceman

He appeared
after five thousand years
under the snow and ice.

We are touched
by his clothes and his tools —
simple, intelligent defenses
to keep himself warm
and manage his way
over the mountains;
and we are troubled to find
the stone arrow,
the arrow that left him
bleeding to death
or freezing to death
after he'd fallen.

Maybe he was innocence
overcome by evil;
maybe he was power
overcome by justice;
or maybe a victim
in the timeless cycle
of revenge begetting revenge.

Whatever happened that day,
he fell,
and all the centuries of snow
preserved him

35

until the day he was found,
still frozen in ice,
like one of us—
reminding us
of who we are.

Identity

A KOAN in the form of a poem.
Buddhist KOAN

In a little book of Buddhist reflections,
I read, "You are not your body,"
and I think I understand its meaning
until I realize all that I am
that I think of
as separate from my body
is all part of my being alive,
and taken together
is my body,
so that if I am
not my body,
who am I?

Who is it who walks?

Inspiration

I took a walk this morning
to look for a poem
down toward the canal
at the end of my street.
The day was cloudy, threatening rain,
unseasonably warm for November.
The last leaves to come down,
huddled together and moving in drifts
on squalls coming in from the north,
made me think I was close
to getting a glimpse of the thing.

At a café table I sat with my coffee
but waited in vain for my poem to appear.
Outside, a dog was tied to a bicycle stand;
I tried to imagine what she was thinking
but nothing came of that either.

When I got to the stairs at the towpath,
it started to rain.
My muse and the ducks—three ladies
and two drakes swimming closely behind,
weren't impressed by the drops
falling on water with the usual concentric effect;
so I went on.

Next came two overpasses, both new,
connecting the buildings on opposite sides,
then three bridges being repaired,
and a quick succession of locks—

all metaphors waiting for someone, no doubt,
but so far, today, not for me.

I was about to go home when it started to pour
so I ducked into a bookshop I liked,
looked around to see what was new.
Billy Collins' *The Trouble with Poetry*,
I'd ordered some time ago, hadn't arrived;
they said it was only a matter of time.
Not a problem I thought;
the trouble with poetry
I was having just now
wasn't waiting for them to find his
but waiting for mine to find me.

It

It was my first day at the Treatment Center
for Alcoholism and Drug Abuse,
and the social worker was telling us
an addict is a person who'll choose
to abandon everything he loves
so he can hold on to his habit.

He may say the choice
depends on something else—
on what is fair,
how he was wronged,
to ease the pain,
to have some fun,
or how the blame is someone else's—
but it all comes down to this:
sooner or later,
the addict always finds a way
to choose his addiction.
Regardless.

He could guarantee us this, he said,
the day will come,
if it hasn't come already,
when you will have to make a choice
between her and it,
or the children and it,
or the parents and it,
or the friends and it,
or your work and it,
even yourself and it,

and it
is what
you'll choose.

I knew he was right —
by now, I'd worked my way
well down his list,
in some cases,
more than once.

It's not a question of whether
but only a question of when, he told us,
that's what addiction is;
so unless you ask for help,
admit you've got a problem
you can't solve on your own,
and try to do better,
the chance it will turn out
some other way is zero.
Even then, I heard him say,
the odds aren't so good.

Though I can't say for sure —
it had been so long ago —
I felt then like I might have felt
the first day of school
shortly after being left:
this was different
from anything I'd done before;

I didn't know what to expect or
how I would do,
and wasn't sure I liked it much;
but I would do it anyway,
at least this one day,
and I've been at it ever since.

Judas Redux

Whether he was a culprit
or just a powerless cog in a cosmic machine,
after reenactments of the Passion,
those who end up hating Judas,
even if only for a moment,
I can understand,
since his kiss of betrayal
sets in motion all that follows:
a story of humiliation, injustice, savagery,
and innocent death.

I'm reminded of George W. Bush kissing
Senator Joe Lieberman at the Capitol
almost two years after
the misbegotten invasion of Iraq
with the nightmare war still going on;
except others, thousands of others—
not Lieberman or the benighted Bush—
are the victims this time
of the latest Middle Eastern crime.

In the Passion,
Judas goes off and hangs himself
in shame and regret afterwards.
The old story would be more like the current one
if, after kissing Jesus,
Judas had gone off to the Palace
and kissed Pontius Pilate instead.

Kindred Spirit

. . .in the woods
a few night birds were calling,
Billy Collins

Once I husked corn with him
out in the long field above the creek,
in the evenings with only a lantern for light.
That was the summer we moved back to the farm
to live with him and my grandmother
after the war was over
and everyone had run into the streets,
unable to contain their joy
when the news was announced.
But now it was October
and the corn fields were the last
to be cleared of their crop.
It was dark when we crossed the wooden bridge
and walked up into the stubbled field
away from the warm light
coming from the windows of the farmhouse.
The stalks had already been chopped
and stacked into shocks
now waiting to be tipped over, then unbundled,
the golden ears stripped of their husks
and thrown into piles one-by-one
as we worked our way down the rows.
In the steady light of the lantern
the full moon rose,
and down in the woods
a few night birds were calling.

Late

Late is
coming or remaining
after the proper time,
or related to
an advanced stage in time;
late is
made, appearing or happening
just before the present time;
late is
far advanced toward the close of day or night;
late is
being something or holding some position
but not now;
late is
living recently,
Syn. DEAD.
Too late.

Slightly edited; from Webster's Seventh New Collegiate
Dictionary

Mating Game

Calaf falls for Turandot.
    Turandot: *Check.*

Calaf plays brilliantly.
    Calaf: *Check.*

Turandot gets another chance,
courtesy of Calaf.
    Turandot: *Check.*

Calaf gets the upper hand again.
    Calaf: *Check.*

But with his final move,
Calaf gives Turandot a choice.

Turandot falls for Calaf.
    Turandot: *Check.*
    Calaf: *Mate.*

Median Strip

It's like I used to be
on that road over there,
going like Hell
flooring it,
seeing what the old baby would do.
And now I'm on this road over here
heading in the opposite direction,
on the other side of the median strip.
And there's no way to get back over
to the other side;
no place to turn around,
no way to get over there again.

How'd I get over here anyway?
I don't remember ever coming over here,
never made a U-turn or anything,
but here I am
headed down this side of the highway
knowing the only place I'm going
is where this road is taking me.
I can change lanes,
pass a car or two,
drop back a car or two.
I can even have a flat.
But I can't turn around.
there's no place to get across the median strip.

What is this median strip?
It's more than dirt and grass and gravel
between two roads.

Euclid would say it's a surface
created by a line in motion,
perpendicular and equidistant from two other lines.
There's also the space above all that.
And time's the part we're in
on either side of the space.

So the median strip's a surface with a space above it,
bounded by time going in opposite directions.

Got it?
OK, here's a question for you:
if space is curved as Einstein says it is,
could I have been to infinity and back?

Morning Mass

Almost every day now
I walk the five blocks from my house —
two blocks south, three blocks west,
then up the steps
to the double doors of the chapel.
A short walk;
if I leave at ten 'til eight
I'm there two minutes early.
On the way,
I pass a house we lived in some years ago,
further along, another
(our numbers were larger then);
I pass my barber shop of twenty years,
and the campus store where I've ordered
countless cups of morning coffee.
Nearing the chapel,
I see young children arriving for school,
some with their parents, some already on their own.
I go in and take my usual seat;
the others, mostly regulars,
are in theirs.
It's never crowded.
The mass is short and always starts on time;
two readings plus the Gospel,
a prayer here and there,
a few words of his own from the priest,
then communion,
the blessing,
and it's over.

Most leave,
but some few stay to pray and say the rosary.
Usually I meditate a while
and especially enjoy
the morning light on sunny days
pouring in the eastern windows.
Then I'm out the doors
and down the steps.
I'm not sure why,
but going home,
like the Magi,
I always take
a different route.

Morning News

At the newspaper box at the end of his street,
an old man drops coins in the slot
like paying Charon for passage.

He opens the door and takes one from the stack,
sees the morning news is not good,
then lets the door close, thinking

the Ancients would have been well-prepared
for their nether world trip,
had they had news and boxes like these.

Mother's Day

It was Mother's Day and some of the kids were fixing
dinner for us over at our daughter Liz's place and I was
watching the O's and the Sox on TV at Fenway after they
split the first two games, the O's taking the first behind
Brian Burres and then losing the second after they pulled
Trachsel in the early innings and brought in Leicester
who the Sox got to right away but Perlozzo left out there
anyway so the bullpen could get some rest, especially
Danys Baez who'd been brilliant in the last couple of
games and probably needed it— even though I hate it
when they write off a game to rest the pen because it's
like giving up in advance and besides it doesn't make a
difference lots of times whether they are rested or not
there are so many other things you can't control going
on in a game that can screw you, and anyway how much
rest do you need after pitching a couple innings of
relief—even if they are on consecutive days. These guys
are athletes aren't they? It's not like running the 440 after
all or any kind of real work but we all know it's all about
the money so much money for an arm that those arms
are like your mother's good china and they get treated
the same way.

Anyway they lost the second game big time and here we
are in the rubber game and a rookie kid named Jeremy
Guthrie is starting for the O's and it's only his second
start in the majors and after a couple of innings of
shutout ball it begins to look like this might be the day
when we take a series from the Sox for the first time
since God knows when (even longer at Fenway) and

after we put a couple of runs on the board, it's looking even better and I start to smile inside. The kid is brilliant I mean brilliant pounding the strike zone and painting the corners so that in the bottom of the ninth with the O's up 5 zip he has a three hit shutout going, one down with a man on first and only two outs away from a complete game with a pitch count still way under 100 and I honestly can't remember if he's even walked a batter. The next guy up hits a little pop up in front of home plate which the catcher gets his glove on but somehow can't hold on to so the batter reaches on an error and with a man on first and second Perlozzo pops out of the dugout I think to give Guthrie a little time to calm down and regroup. But what's this? He's pulling Guthrie! Sammy how can you do it?! This kid has given it everything he's got! He's put it all on the line Sammy and you're pulling him? Shame, Sammy, shame. If you have to take somebody out for God's sake, take out the catcher! He's the one who dropped the ball! This kid's earned the right to finish what he started. But Perlozzo has the right to make the call and he brings in Baez to finish off the Sox, the well-rested Baez, the experienced Baez, the Baez who's pitched nearly perfect ball in his last three relief appearances. So Guthrie gives the ball to Perlozzo and gets a hand from the Sox fans as he exits.

Then things turn ugly. Very ugly. Baez comes in and allows a double and a single to the first two batters he faces and a run scores putting the Sox down 5-1 and runners on first and third. Rest or no Baez doesn't have it today and so Perlozzo brings in his closer who has been almost foolproof. The closer walks the first two batters he faces driving in another run, and then with the bases still loaded the next batter rips a hit into right center scoring two more runs and the score is now 5-4 with runners on second and third. The next batter is intentionally walked to load the bases to set up a force at any base which the O's get at home. Now with two out and the bases still loaded, the next batter puts down a soft little infield hit between first and second which the first baseman takes and tosses to the pitcher covering first for the final out. But the play is close and the pitcher bobbles the ball! The runner is safe, two runs score and the Sox take it 6-5. The Sox fans go crazy. I go crazy. For an instant I understand why murder and madness often go together. It's all Perlozzo's fault and I want to *get* Perlozzo! Somewhere in my mind I know he was just trying to win the game and save the win for Guthrie if he could and that the odds are the move he made was right. But it's no use. Somewhere else in my mind I know there are times when you have to say fuck the odds, fuck the arm, fuck the mother's china, and go for the glory. Sure maybe they lose if Perlozzo leaves him in. But they lose anyway when Perlozzo takes him out, lose the chance to do something really great regardless of the final score.

For hours I'm so totally disgusted and outraged I'm not fit to be around. My wife wants to know why I'm so miserable and why this game is bothering me so much and I tell her I'm tired of them always figuring the odds, tired of them going with what they figure, tired of losing anyway, but somehow still can't let go of it, so I put on the game face and go to dinner and when she asks me again later when we get home how I'm doing I tell her I'm straightening myself out a little because I'm thinking

54

how Perlozzo must feel right now like the five star French chef who committed suicide after he discovered the fish he'd served was bad and maybe Perlozzo will do the same. But it wasn't until that evening I'm reading some poems of Bukowski and I come across the lines "Immortality can be a very/brief experience," that it hits me: pitching a game like that is one of the few grand things in life and it's still grand even if you don't get to finish it, even if the bastards take you out before you're ready, take you out while you still have something in the tank. At my age, I better know this and I do but I don't always remember it. Thanks, Chinaski, for reminding me.

Mower

Across the road a horn is honking;
I go outside to see why.
My grandfather is lying in the grass
near the gnarled apple tree,
the old push-mower next to him.
I shout and my father comes.
We carry him inside
and lay him on the couch.
My mother calls the doctor.
The doctor comes
but nothing can be done.
We sit with death
until the black van comes for him.
Outside, in the unfinished yard,
astride the path that he was on,
the mower waits,
arm extended like a benediction
over the swath behind,
as if unconcerned
about the uncut swath ahead.

Nicene Creed

I used to say this
on the Sundays I went to church,
thinking—when I thought at all—
it summed up fairly well and in brief
my Christian faith,
what it was I believed in.
But somewhere along the line,
unfortunately, or perhaps not,
I started examining more carefully
the words I was saying
and questioning whether I *truly* believed them.
I think "resurrection of the dead"
were the first words to go,
then "Virgin Birth,"
and it wasn't long until
pretty much everything else
theological was gone
and I was down to "One God
[no Father, no Almighty],
Creator of Heaven and Earth,
of all that is seen and unseen."
These words seemed unexceptionable
and things were fine for awhile.
But there was a problem:
I couldn't get the questions stopped
so now I'm even having doubts about them.
As I look around me,
I have to admit that the Creation—
the Big Bang, if you wish—

and what has followed,
has all the earmarks of being
the work of a committee, a committee
whose factions couldn't agree
on how the world should be,
which perhaps explains
why we have light *and* dark,
life *and* death, good *and* evil,
do's *and* don'ts, and
the very slippery concept of free-will,
and all the other mishmash
of what we usually associate
with democratic sovereignty
rather than the strict authority
of autocratic rule.

Nirvana

If it's
true,
as Sartre
once said,
we are
what we
do,
and
if it's
true
there is
nothing
we can
do
about our
death,
then,
when we
take
our
last
breath,
for
(at least)
that moment,
aren't
we
nothing
too?

On Love

When love blooms
for Emile DeBecque and Ensign Nellie Forbush
in the middle of a war,
on a small island in the South Pacific
both happened to have landed on,

some say the encounter—
what happened across that crowded room—
and what follows,
is all about the role of chance,
and how the unpredictable element in our lives,
rules our lives.

But for those of us who've fallen—
on some enchanted evening or otherwise—
I think it's fair to say
the feel of it is more like certainty than uncertainty,
more like destiny than just a random pretty face,

or, put another way,
more like Newton's gravity
than Heisenberg's famous principle.

For us, love, like gravity,
seems always on the mark;
and like a spring waiting to uncoil,
always ready to leap into our lives,
and always does—
when given the chance,
and we take it.

Palm Sunday

The first year he said it,
I'm betting the week was full of promise:
a bright sun
in the midst of mild spring days,
daffodils in bloom
like a friendly crowd watching a parade go by,
narrow waving leaves of early budding willows,
the reappearance of the mourning doves,
maybe even children's laughter
coming from an open farmhouse window.

Though it wasn't like that first year every year,
every year it was—
when all our senses told us
winter's bitter cold was over,
Grandpa would warn us once again:
Don't go overboard, he'd say,
*I remember weather just like this
not many years ago,
the week before we got a foot of snow
on Palm Sunday.*

Pick and Roll

Well-guarded,
his teammate dribbles
cross-court
just beyond the arc—
the big man comes out
and sets the pick
while his teammate
dribbles on
briefly screened
from his defender.
In the next split-second,
the big man pivots
then rolls toward
the basket where he
can take a pass
and stuff it
or let his teammate,
if he's open,
drill one
on his own.

It's not a metaphor
for anything
but it's poetry
just the same.

Pigs

In the nursery game there are five,
one for each toe on your foot,
but in my grandfather's pen,
the number was two,
bought at the livestock auction each spring,
beloved through summer and fall,
and into deep midwinter.
Fattened on ground corn and milk we called mash,
table scraps and other goodies
like apples and potato peels they seemed to love,
along with vegetables from our garden,
eggs from our chickens and milk from our cows—
their ribs, chops, bacon, hams, and sausage
was mostly what we lived on.

The dreaded moment in this pattern came,
always on a bitter cold morning,
when my grandfather would take his rifle to the pen
instead of their food.
Not only was no one else allowed to go with him,
he insisted everyone also stay inside the house;
but still we couldn't help but hear
the first shot from the .22,
and then the terror of the second pig
screaming for her life:
we heard no desire for her master's love,
no desire for food, friendship of man or other beast,
nothing but the overriding fear of imminent death
and the pure desire to stay alive.

Then we heard the second shot
and all the screaming stopped
which everyone was glad for;
and after that the day looked like
it could have been a scene from Bruegel
of Dutch peasants five hundred years before:
the big, iron kettles over open fires,
the two 10' wooden tripods
and the disemboweled pigs
hanging by their rear feet,
upside down, white and naked,
already scraped clean of their bristles,
the long wooden tables
set up for the remaining work,
knives sharp and ready
for the family, friends, and neighbors
who came to help.

Soon all seemed to forget how the day began —
the brief reign of terror put behind them —
but when the work was done
and we went in for supper,
I don't remember ever eating any meat
but rather turnips, green beans, and beets
from the cold cellar we always called the Cave,
a relic of some French or German ancestor
who'd owned the place years before.
And later being sent up to bed
and crawling between the heavy covers
in my cold, unheated room,
wondering what it's like to die,
wondering when the master comes,
whether it's better to be like
the first pig or the second.

Quilting

Every Wednesday,
except in summer when we were out of school,
my mother and her women friends from church
served an inexpensive noon-day meal
at the village hall of the Redman's Lodge
to any and all who came—many regulars,
some just in the neighborhood who happened by—
to help with costs not covered by
the church collections taken
every Sunday.

When the meal was done and while
the cleaning up was still going on,
the wooden frames would come out
with the trestles that they rested on,
and the quilt in progress on the frames
would be unrolled.

The appliqués of bright-colored scraps of cloth,
sewn together in a variety of shapes—
a flower or a heart, sometimes a circle or a square,
sometimes a different geometry instead—
first were fastened to the larger piece of cloth
that would become the top half of the quilt,
then cotton batting was spread on the lower half
and quilting the two halves together would begin,
the stitched designs of the quilters following
the lines lightly penciled on the cloth.

When I was a boy, the quilting seemed
just a special art,
not one my mother liked, as I recall;
sewing up the appliqués was more her speed
she always said.

Now the quilting seems like many other things:
the needle, like desire,
guided by the eye and hand above,
positioned by the finger of the unseen hand below,
piercing the layers of cloth and batting,
the sharp tip appearing and disappearing,
over and over,
connecting the two halves,
stitching them together;
and after each stitch is snugged,
the pause, like two lovers resting;

the stitches so tiny and so numerous,
each like a day,
and the thread, like time,
connecting all the days together;
fate, the penciled lines;
and the quilt in progress
stretched between the frames,
like a vast map of battlefields
in a theatre of war.

Rocinante

When Don Quixote saddled up Rocinante,
he saw a horse like Kemo Sabe's Silver
or Trigger, Roy's golden palomino—
a trick played on him by a mind gone mad.
Surely Rocinante had no illusions
of her beauty or her goodness
but also knew
she had no choice
but to play along.
So are we also often cast by others
and often also we go along
knowing the truth of our predicament:
to live someone else's dream of us
or the reality of our swaying back
and skinny legs.
But after all the windmills
have been tilted
and our knight in armor
lay crashed upon the ground,
we do allow ourselves to wander off
and graze quietly in the meadow,
there, just below the windmill turrets,
just beyond the whirring blades.

Steel Pier

It was the summer weekend I went to Atlantic City
with my steady girlfriend and her parents,
long before the casinos,
the Trump Taj Mahal and all that;
the attractions then were the ocean,
the sand and the boardwalk—
the wide, pedestrian-only, wood-paved boulevard
that seemed like a fresh-air version
of Times Square on one side
with the beach on the other.

What I remember most about that weekend though
was not any of those things,
but on Saturday night hearing Gene Krupa
play drum solos in the Marine Ballroom
out at the end of Steel Pier.
The Pier jutted out into the ocean surf
at right angles to the boardwalk
and in those days was its biggest attraction.
It was just opposite the rooftop Planter's Peanut sign
and the outsized Mr. Peanut,
with top hat, monocle, and cane,
seemed almost like a maitre d'
showing everyone in.

Krupa had made quite a splash there years before
when he got his first real taste of fame,
but now he was a jazz star of long standing
and everyone was full of anticipation
about hearing the great Chicago Flash.

Hearing him play was like hearing
the sound of another world:
part mind, part intuition,
like the music of a man's soul.
No one had ever heard anyone
so close to the skins before
or hotter with the sticks.

The band played for a while before he came on
and some couples danced,
but when Krupa started playing
the dancing stopped
and everyone gathered around him
to watch and to listen.

The music filled the ballroom
and made the sand and sea,
the boardwalk and the Steel Pier itself,
seem unimportant.
All that mattered was to be there for the man
and the deep sounds and pounding rhythms —
like an incantation coming from his drums.

There may have been a spotlight on Krupa,
though I don't recall it;
even the crowd seemed to recede into the shadows
and all the space was filled
with the music of an unseen world,
like the thundering horses of the Apocalypse
riding out the world
until the end of time.

Still Life

This morning I'm at my usual table
with notebook and pen,

looking at the solitary shakers of pepper and salt,
glass with chrome tops

like a pair of lost chessmen,
one black, one white,

next to a small container of sweeteners,
the multi-colored packets fitting exactly,

and in a slender bud vase, also of glass,
a few stems of half-opened carnations

and a sprig of white baby's breath,
all on a background of gray vinyl.

A woman seated at the window sketching on a pad
looks away when I look at her,

pausing in her work as I write down,
Old man with coffee in local café.

Ten Lines

In the bookstore Men's Room stall,
the wall ahead was pale yellow
but the side panels were deep, dark green.
Standing there I couldn't help but notice
there was no graffiti,
no sexual graphics,
no numbers inviting me to call.
A fresh coat of paint, I thought;
but peripheral vision being what it is,
something on my right seemed to disagree,
and turning just my head a bit in that direction
I saw there were some scratches
on the new green paint after all.
Honestly, I couldn't make them out at first;
what I thought I saw —
a Chinese character scratched out quickly —
seemed unlikely I admit,
and sure enough,
looking closer,
it wasn't calligraphy of any kind;
just two lines like finger-nail moons
lying on their sides,
a small, wiggly circle of a line
centered on each one;
two concave lines made
a narrow-waisted lower torso;
then two long arching lines,
definitely two thighs spread apart;
and below them two shorter convex lines
intersecting, then joined together at one end,

making both a . . .
well, you know.
It really wasn't bad for what it was;
a few sure, quick strokes capturing an essence,
a Men's Room Matisse or even a Picasso.
The Jolly Green Giant in just ten lines, I thought,
a different sort of giant
but a giant just the same.
and then I thought,
Ho, ho, ho.
And after washing up and returning to the store
to find what I was looking for,
the thought occurred to me how right it was
the last laugh should be hers.

near drowning experience

Tolchester Secrets

In 1946, Tolchester was home
to a modest beach amusement park
on the Eastern Shore across the Bay from Baltimore;
day-trippers took the ferry there from the city,
and on this day, the boy, his mother, and his aunt were
among them.

The boy couldn't swim.
After they'd changed
and spread their blanket on the beach,
his mother let him go into the water on his own
warning him not to go out too far
and to stay where she could watch him,

a warning he ignored when he saw
she was distracted, talking to his aunt.
On out he went, confident he could always
turn around and return to shore when he wished
or even swim if he wanted to;
there couldn't be that much to it, or so he thought.

Soon though, he was on his tiptoes
and then a moment came when a current
retreating from the shore carried him out too far,
and he felt his feet swept off the sandy bottom
and the thought that he could drown
pierced his mind.

He couldn't shout —
his mouth was under water;

and he couldn't jump because
there was nothing to push off from;
and he couldn't wave because
his hands were busy paddling frantically.

What he saw as he went under
were the people in the water all around him,
people who could save him if he could call for help,
if he could share his plight. But he knew he couldn't;
drowning was like having a secret he couldn't share, a
secret he couldn't tell anyone about.

And then, as fate would have it,
a random current pushed him back toward shore,
and the next instant he felt his toes
touch the sandy bottom.
He pushed hard, broke through the watery ceiling,
breathed,

went under,
and pushed off again several times,
each time projecting himself shoreward
until he was safe once more in shallow water,
his mother and his aunt nearby,
neither aware of what had happened.

Only a few minutes had gone by
but it seemed to him much longer,
like a slow, different kind of time,
and his mother and his aunt
seemed different too somehow,
as if he'd never seen them in that distant way before,

like far away strangers almost,
and when he heard the noise
and sounds of pleasure going on around him,
that was different too,
like sounds he was hearing for the first time,
as if he'd never really heard them either.

Then he lay down on the blanket,
warmed by the sun above and the sand below,
thinking only of how good it felt
and how glad he was to be there.

And after a while, they all went back into the water,
with him holding his mother's hand on one side
and his aunt's on the other
and to his surprise, he was happy for it.

Odd, he thought, that he should be
remembering all this now,
approaching his sixty-ninth year,

mother and aunt long dead, the beach deserted,
the amusement park in ruins,
feeling again something of what he was feeling then,

remembering with both pleasure and regret
she never guessed that day what happened
and he'd never told her.

Two Vultures

I was surprised to see them on the church tower,
one perched on the rail of the balustrade,
the other on the masonry ball atop a corner post,
two vultures,

outlined against a blue expanse of springtime sky,
surveying the surrounding countryside,
inspecting the greening fields and pastures
for the dying and the dead.

The cars parked around the church
said the service inside was still going on,
and coming closer I could hear,
through the open doors,

the congregation sing a hymn,
then the rumble of the Creed, and afterwards,
a few words from the Gospel,
and some of the homily.

How much the birds could understand
is hard to know,
though there was a point
when the preacher said,

"Dying you shall live,"
when I happened to look up,
and—maybe I imagined it—thought I saw
their hooded eyes exchange a knowing glance.

Us

The news coming in is so bad, all the time,
from every part of the known world,
I have to think these are not isolated events at all
but part of a much bigger story being totally missed
by those reporting on them,

like a daily rendering of the misery
of each pair of animals aboard the Ark—
the forced voyage, the unrelenting rain,
the cramped quarters, the stale air, the boring food,
the strange bedfellows—

but never a word about the Flood.

Or like a program on public TV
about the mass extinction of every form of dinosaur
some sixty-five million years ago,
but no mention of the six-mile-wide asteroid
striking planet Earth—

just before the end of *T. Rex* and all his kind.

Vermeer

The leitmotifs in his paintings—
the wine carafe,
oak table and table rug,
map or painting
hanging on the background wall,
the geometry of his composition,
the radiant light
coming through the leaded glass,
the preternatural colors—
all hint at his meaning
and who the master is.
His motifs—
of women,
usually alone or in pairs,
reading letters,
weighing pearls,
pouring milk,
making lace—
intend to illustrate a vice
or celebrate a virtue,
like vanity or too much wine,
adultery, sometimes sloth,
or modesty and useful work
(this is Calvinist Holland after all);
but regardless of the message,
in all their faces,
and those of his few men as well,

there is no guilt or dread,
suffering or doubt,
no contumely,
but always,
unmistakably,
somehow,
pleasure.

Waiting

Here I am,
like an obedient
dog
commanded to
stay, or an
actor
between takes
while
the movie's
director
sets up
his next shot.
Here I am,
sitting at
Kay Ryan's
table
floating down
the Niagara
River, now
close enough
to hear
the roar,
remembering
what it means.

Washington Evening

*He talked a lot about the past and I gathered that he wanted to
recover something, some idea of himself perhaps that had gone
into loving Daisy.*

F. Scott Fitzgerald, *The Great Gatsby*

One of my most vivid memories of Washington
is an open-air performance of the ballet,
A Midsummer-Night's Dream,
at Carter Barron Amphitheatre in Rock Creek Park,
that first summer here, an evening
many, many years ago.

Edward Villella of the New York City Ballet
starred as Oberon;
I don't recall
who danced the role of Titania
or any of the others' names.

But I do remember when
the four mysterious chords
of Mendelssohn's Overture sounded
and then gave way to the evanescent fairy music —
the notes like twinkling snowflakes
falling in a shimmering world of darkness
lit only by a winter moon,

the past was, for a moment,
like a time I couldn't remember
and I was being ferried away
on the wings of a magic bird
to a wondrous place and time

where a new life would begin for us,
with new sweet triumphs
and new failures too,
and I was suddenly, unutterably,
aware of my connection to all that is
and was to come,
and my place in it,
once again.

Weather

*About
Chaos theory*

I often sit out here on warm, sunny days,
reading the paper with my morning coffee
while the other patrons take their turns
going in and coming out the café doors
opening to the narrow sidewalk.

And this morning is no different:

here we are
all of us pretty harmless I'd say,
including the well-behaved Rottweiller
tied to the bicycle stand with eyes and a forehead
that remind me of Shakespeare's,

the college student in flip-flops at the next table
checking his cell phone for incoming calls,
and even the cars maneuvering around
the double-parked beer truck
making deliveries.

But Edward Lorenz, 90, who died yesterday,
thought differently I learn from the story I'm reading,
a meteorologist who discovered by accident
how very small changes in one place
can trigger very big changes elsewhere,

and famously showed —
though for years his work was largely ignored —
how the flop of a butterfly's wing in Brazil,

83

by a process scientifically modeled,
could set off a tornado in Texas.

Though clever enough,
most scientists thought it could not be literally true,
but it turned out it could, the story says,
with dramatic results as important for science
as relativity theory and quantum mechanics.

Not bad, I think, for a professor at MIT
who only wanted to understand why
it's so hard to forecast the weather,
though as meteorologists go,
the man on local TV is likely known better.

We're often reminded these days
how important it is to get out of ourselves,
to rise above our personal, even inconsequential lives,
to get beyond our trivial pursuits,
to count for something, make a real difference.

But the way I see it Lorenz was telling us
the dog wagging his tail could be just as important,
so too, the kid texting someone over his phone,
or the driver dodging the beer truck,
or me stirring my coffee,

that the very least of our actions,
even writing this poem,
can leave its mark on the world—
perhaps a late snowfall in Denver next week
or a typhoon in Bali the week after that.

Wheel

Once upon a time,
in a blue, two-door '39 Ford
with stick shift
and bench seats,
a little boy riding in back,
like Miss Daisy,
with his Mom and Dad in front,
amused himself watching
the turning wheels of trucks
they passed.
At first, all was just a spinning blur
until he noticed the lug nuts
near the center of a wheel
turned more slowly than the tire.
It puzzled him for a while
how the lugs,
making the same number of turns,
but going at a slower speed,
could get to the same destination as the tire
in the same amount of time.
After all, even at his tender age
he knew speed x time = distance.
Finally, it occurred to him
the rotation of the lugs accounted for
only a portion of the total distance traveled
by the wheel.
As for the rest, the lugs were being carried
by the tire—
the wheel's only part to make the trip
entirely on its own.

He guessed that a tiny, tiny dot
at the very center of the wheel
was carried all the way.

He couldn't have been much more than ten
when first he figured all this out.
Now, years later,
he thought he should have somehow done
much more with it.

Why a Vineyard?

is a question
I'm often asked.
I used to say
it's like playing golf—
but a lot of people I know
don't play golf
and as it turns out
neither do I.
So now I say
it's like being a pianist
of modest means
with some modest talent,
but one lucky enough
to own a grand piano:
a beautiful thing to have
and an even greater pleasure
to play on.
I'm almost never asked
if I play—
which is good,
because I don't play piano
either.

Why a Vineyard? Part 2

I used to think that owning a vineyard
was a lot like playing golf
but then gave up that image
in favor of playing on a grand piano
in one's own living room.
Now I'm thinking that playing golf
was closer to correct,
with the golfer pitted against the course—
the tricky greens, the traps, the trees,
the water—beautiful to look at,
like the grand,
but much more of an opponent,
like the vineyard.

The latest challenge up here is eutypa dieback,
which sounds like the name of some character
from a southern, romance novel
(old Miss Eutypa Dieback,
never married, lives alone, relatives all dead),
but instead is a nasty fungus that first infects
the vine's woody tissue in the cordon arms,
and after killing them, if left unchecked,
works its way over to and down the trunk,
then into the roots, and kills everything else.

Today, I have to add it to last year's drought,
and before that the grapeberry moth,
the late frost, the lightning strikes, the hurricane;
plus the yearly pests:
the birds, the deer, the Japanese beetles;

and the constant threats: botrytis, downy mildew,
powdery mildew, black rot, bunch rot,
phomopsis and all the other ills vines are heir to.

Sometimes a vineyard makes you feel
like Rafael Nadal looked this morning
on the front page of the Sports section
after beating Roger Federer
in five sets in 4 hours and 48 minutes
of championship play at Wimbledon:
flat on his back, spread-eagled,
exhausted, completely drained.
But don't think I'm going to say
a vineyard's like tennis; it's not.
After all, Nadal did *win*.

Somehow I'm led back to baseball
and a game I watched recently:
after the starting pitcher threw eight complete innings
of nearly shutout ball and allowing only one run,
he was taken out by the manager still leading 2 to 1
in favor of the closer
who came on in the top of the ninth
and allowed the opposing team to tie,
sending the game into extra innings
after his own team failed to score
in the bottom of the ninth.
But that wasn't the end of it.
The closer was the pitcher of record
when his team went ahead in a later inning;
so the closer got the win
even though he blew the save
and the starter got a no decision.

When asked about it afterwards,
the manager said, "That's baseball,"
and after watching many more games
than I care to admit, I have to agree.

It's also a lot like growing grapes.

Winter Light

nice winter observation

From my small room
I look out this morning on the winter garden.
In the rear, away from the house
a single tree, an ornamental cherry,
like a woman of a certain age,
spreads its limbs
looking for the light.
As the sun rises over my house,
first the topmost branches,
then the larger limbs,
and finally the trunk,
are bathed in descending light.
As the world continues turning east
each part of the tree enters the growing shadow
of my neighbor's house
until only the tip of one small branch
reaching toward the sky,
once the first to brighten,
becomes the last to dim
in the ascending darkness.

X

There's the one that marks the spot,
the one that makes me think
of where the treasure's buried.
There's the one in Xmas
for the first letter of Christ's name in Greek;
speaking of which reminds me
of the Roman numeral ten.
Of course we can't forget the kisses
at the bottom Joe Young wrote about
and Fats Waller sounded
oh so glad to get.
And finally, there's the symbol for
the unknown quantity
you're introduced to
when you get to Middle School.

Just when you've mastered all of arithmetic,
you walk into the classroom
and the teacher, mine was male,
writes an equation on the board
and you're told to solve for x.
There were a few, right then and there,
who knew they would be English majors;
but the rest, like me,
did it fine by trial and error,
because it wasn't really hard for us to do.

As he made the problems tougher though
that method didn't work so well
and when we at last gave up on it,

he showed us how to do it right.
"Put all the 'knowns' on one side of the equals sign
and all the 'unknowns' on the other,"
he said, and used arithmetic to do it.

I remember it was fun —
once we got the hang of it —
making sure what we did on one side
was what we did on the other,
perhaps a little taste of power
playing in this algebraic world,
solving for the unknown quantity;
not unlike the feeling I had a few years later
close dancing at the Junior Prom:
after a little bit of trial and error,
learning how to do it right,
then having the fun of solving for x.

Yellow Leaves

In Fall,
the leaves of aspens
some azaleas
birch
gingko
some varieties of grapes
hosta
some phlox
poplars
and wisteria
to name just a few
all have yellow leaves
as if they share
some ancient
common ancestry
like yellow hair
some cat's eyes
a Yukon Gold potato
and a harvest moon.

Zen Dog

My theory is Tibetan monks
learned Zen from dogs,
Tibetan terriers to be precise,
a dog like mine.

Serene as the Dali Lama,
she doesn't mind
when other dogs come over;
she sits or lays stretched out
ignoring them completely,
paws extended front and back,
eyes fixed on the wall,
meditating quietly,
on what
we do not know.

On a trip to see my uncle,
she took up her position in the yard
and didn't even seem to notice
his Jack Russell
racing all around her
yapping, flapping,
jumping, growling,
stopping right in front of her,
poised as if he was going to pounce.
She deigned to look him in the eye
but only for a moment
before she turned her head
to gaze once more
at something in the middle distance,

and the little dog gave up, exhausted,
and went into the house.

Figuring she might like going to church,
I took her once to evening mass.
It was confirmation, the church was full
and the bishop, with his retinue,
was there in full regalia.
We came late and had to stand in back
just inside the double doors
opened to the warm, spring night.
Unimpressed with all the pomp and circumstance,
she sat quietly on the threshold,
her back squarely to the altar,
nose pointed to the stars.
And while the rest of us
attended to our own creations,
she scoped out the heavens
looking there it seemed
for something else.

II.

Anniversary

Lasting love is. . .a gentleman's game.
Annie Dillard, *The Maytrees*

I.

With all due respect to Ms. Dillard,
truly, when I hear her words,
I'm not reminded of golf or tennis,

or even soccer—a gentleman's game,
according to the British,
played by thugs,

nor am I reminded of sportsmanship,
dash, measured response, cultivated style,
or elaborate notions of grace under pressure,

but rather of W. C. Fields in *My Little Chickadee*,
a con-artist in a stovepipe hat playing high card
who first refuses a look at the other man's cut

then cuts for himself and claims he's the winner,
takes the money but never shows his own card
and pronounces it all a gentleman's game.

II.

Years ago,
while celebrating an early anniversary,
I remember you saying,

101

"It seems like a lifetime,"
and both of us laughed
over what you really meant:

true mates whose lives together
crowded out the loves we'd known before,
or,

two people in a tiresome marriage
as loveless as an odd sock,
and just as useless and forlorn.

III.

Now, here we are, years later—
our lives together much nearer
to your old summary of it all—

and lasting love seems more like a set of skills,
like a trade or craft we slowly learn
to make a work worth being part of,

although whether what we've made
is art or otherwise
could be a matter of opinion.

I suppose science will someday
find ways to measure it all,
but for now it's more a sense of rightness

we must rely on,
or, as my grandfather,
a sometime farmer and carpenter,

used to say,
"If it looks right,
it *is* right."

IV.

So today, our anniversary,
we, like him,
stand back from the fence posts we've planted,

and the doors we've hung,
moving first to one side
and then the other,

eyeing our work,
comparing the result with some perfect
but invisible standard in our hearts

and, with at least a dash of humility
and an equal measure of gratitude,
are pleased with what we see.

Aubade

Pale streams of light are seeping into dawn,
Birds now waking in warm nests, greet the morn,
Deep in woods a doe eyes her sleeping fawn
And woodland roses prick the air with thorns.
Rising sun o'er all spreads a golden fleece
That warms our souls and fills the world with peace.
We wake together as the hour begins
Knowing time and chance rule the coming day.
But naught matters if, on this morning gray
We must part, if, ere long, we meet again.

Bookcases

Bookcases like a man and woman stand
beside the hearth as one on either hand;
and from their shelves the albums we take down
recall to us the life in which we're bound:
events now past and seldom brought to mind,
the play, the work, and joy we strove to find,
when every day was like the one before,
the next a happy dream of nothing more.
Now the winter days are fast approaching,
the fire is lit to warm the night again;
the glowing flames reflecting from the wall
remind us both the one is there for all;
old volumes side-by-side the shelves have filled,
comforting like the fire between us still.

Choices

Frost claims he took the road less traveled
and we have to assume he did.
But did he have a choice?
Even if he stood there deliberating,
looking like he could go either way,
could he?

Sometimes as I am drifting off to sleep
I wonder how it was I got here,
in this house, on this street, in this city,
in bed with this woman,
a man born on a farm outside Baltimore,
a woman born in New York five years later;
all the steps that brought us closer:
the schools we attended,
how we came here when school was over,
the jobs we had,
the different marriages,
how we met, fell in love,
the children,
and so on—
how each choice I made wasn't like a choice at all
but like a natural consequence of all the others,
and all those were like that too,
all the way back;
and everyone else, I thought, even Frost,
shared the same fate.

So that being here tonight in this bed
was as inevitable as the setting of the sun today or
its rising in the morning;
that what appeared to be a choice
was just a concatenation of circumstances
I didn't control
except I happened to be there too,
and wanted to be happy.

Chris's Car

For Matthew

When something can't be found
and you ask him where it is,
chances are he'll say,
"It's in the back of Chris's car."

When I consider all that car must hold —
the wrenches alone are daunting:
socket (metric and non-)
adjustable, open-ended, monkey and pipe,
and all the other missing tools;
then there are the belts, pants, shirts,
socks and shoes,
underwear, hats, coats, gloves, jackets, and scarves,
watches, wallets, and keys,
books and backpacks,
sunglasses, cell phones (and chargers),
duffle bags of dirty clothes,
laptops and CD's,
and God knows what else —
I believe a small department store
could be made of it
or even something more ambitious,
if it had household appliances,
you know, washers and dryers
and things like that,
and maybe it does.

Out of college now,
soon the day will come

when Virginia Woolf's dream
of an independent income
and a room of her own to go with it
comes true for him.

On that day
the moving van won't back up to our house
to load his things and take them to his new abode.
I didn't see it quite this way before
but realize now he's been moving out right along,
and all he'll have to do
is call his old friend to come over,
hop in,
drive away,
and then unload
what's already in the back
of Chris's car.

Christmas Visit from the Grandchildren

No one can do it really—
write a good poem about it—
and even if they could,
no one would read it—

the subject too commonplace,
the feelings too ordinary,
the ho-hum poem,
the mundane poem everyone skips,

the one which starts with their arrival
on a day not long after Christmas,
the noise on the front porch
already disturbing the peace,

their parents with shopping bags
loaded with presents not far behind,
all part of the script
for this time of year,

then opening the door,
their bursting inside
full of spark and pep
like ponies gone wild,

then the familiar hugging and kissing,
the hoisting aloft,
and the brief bit of shyness
before we're connected again,

and soon the presents come out,
then the usual cookies and tea
in front of the fire,
the long afternoon,

the stories we've all heard,
maybe some new ones as well,
the laughter and
too many people talking at once,

the going off to play games of their own,
the dark outside closing in,
their Mother protesting it's late,
everyone getting ready to go,

the coats on again
the reloaded bags,
the going out the door,
the returning quiet —

no, it can't be done,
no matter how dedicated the poet,
or even how talented,
it's just out of reach —

how we spend our lives,
one minute gathering our world together
and the next minute,
taking it all apart —

and that's the story for this one as well,
and if you've come this far,
which is doubtful,
you know by now what I mean.

Clowns

Of each other, we should be kind
While there is still time.
                    Philip Larkin

A little more than halfway through his life,
Edward Hopper painted *Lighthouse on a Hill*,
a sunlit, hilly landscape in the foreground,
like a sea with undulating waves of light and shadow,
a house and lighthouse on the crest,
beyond, nothing but the sky.

The angle Hopper chose—
looking at his subject from below—
is the same for *The Comedians*,
completed thirty-eight years later,
but the subject is two people,
a man and woman.

In other works of his I've seen,
the hands of Hopper's couples never touch,
as if each man, each woman
is closed off from the other.

But in this his final picture,
the two clowns not only hold each other's hands
but with their free hand
proffer the other to the audience;
a man and woman take their final bow,
near the front of the proscenium,
the light in front of them,
only the dark, closed curtain behind.

Dated Stones

I had searched throughout the day,
crossed and re-crossed the road
from Riva to Prince Frederick,
on old byways, looking for the stones
of my ancestors, Christopher and Ann.

In 1661, from Bristol, England
they had come, a hundred-sixty years
before the Bateman's son, William, married Sally,
a daughter born five generations later
to their great, great, great grandson, Tom.

And now I'd found them,
here in the cemetery of old St. James Church,
Episcopal, Herring Creek Parish,
at 1665 and 1675, thought to be
the oldest dated stones in Maryland.

All the headstones then were much the same,
like the two in front of me,
side by side,
little file tabs in the ground
marking the lives of those below.

Except they weren't below;
just the stones had been moved there
according to the plaque,
(from a field across the road
I later learned.)

I wondered if those who moved them knew
these two were Quaker émigrés
looking for a friendly shore,
after years of persecution and some time in jail
for refusing to accept

the Church of England as supreme
in all things religious—
the very same Church which built St. James
across the road from where they lay
some years after they had died.

I couldn't help thinking how
the ghosts of Christopher and Ann had felt
the day they saw their stones were gone:
certainly surprised; and even more surprised
when they discovered where they were.

Desert Flowers

Years ago now,
after flying out to Phoenix for his sister's funeral,
we stopped in Albuquerque on our way back east,
my father and I,
and rented a car
for a day-trip to the famous Laboratory
where the atomic age incubated,
before being born in the New Mexico desert,
like a flower,
with Oppenheimer looking on.

That was the day we were out there in the high desert
on our drive north to Los Alamos,
surrounded by flowers of a different sort,
vast drifts of blue and yellow as far as one could see,
so overpowering, even a man like my father,
a man not usually given to appreciation
of the finer points of roadside flowers,
wanted to stop, get out,
and stand for a while
in the midst of them.

Now, even more years from Almagordo,
after many more trips like that one,
my wife and I are coming home again—
this time it was her uncle—
and from the window of the train,
we can see the invading fragmites,
beautiful too,
but in a different way than desert flowers,
spreading across the Jersey meadowlands,

looking like they reach
the far-distant skyline of Manhattan
whose shore we cannot see.

As the train continues south from New York,
we take comfort in the presence of the other,
as if we didn't know the day will likely come
when one of us will be coming home alone,
uncertain which of us it will be,
maybe looking out the window of a car
at desert flowers, or fragmites
flying by from the window of a train like this,
pulling one of us home,
making stops at Trenton, Philadelphia,
Wilmington, and Baltimore,
until it stops for good.

Easy Rider

For Robert

The Big Wheel was the 1970's version of the tricycle.
The whole thing was made of plastic
except for some minor hardware here and there.

You sat low to the ground
between the wide rear wheels
and because the diameter of the front wheel,
the wheel that gave the toy its name,
was four times greater than the other two,
you reached up to the handle bars when you rode
like Peter Fonda did in *Easy Rider*,
your feet stretched out in front to work the pedals—
very cool if you are of a certain age.

I remember him riding it
down the hill of our driveway
and out into the cul de sac our house was on,
then pedaling back to the driveway
and pushing it up the hill,
turning around in the carport
and heading back down again.
Up and down, over and over,
as if he would never stop—
like he was doing something necessary,
something that he had to do.

That was thirty years ago.
Even then it brought to mind the myth of Sisyphus—
forced to roll that stone up the hill forever,

only to have it roll back down
and then having to start all over again.

Thinking about it now though,
I could see there were important differences:
the Big Wheel wasn't heavy like the rock;
also, he could stop when he wanted to
and ride back down instead of walk.

Still, the mythic image stuck, wouldn't go away
until at last it came to me:
had the ancient Greeks had Big Wheels,
this would be like the myth of Sisyphus the Kid.

Flagpole

I have this image of a little girl,
standing by the flagpole,
waiting,
in a smocked summer dress,
trying to imagine
why she had been left;
what could have happened to the father
who had said he would come for her
but hadn't.

What were her thoughts?
Had he forgotten,
or more important things to do?
Had she not been good,
and for that was he going to leave her there?
Should she wait,
or start to walk,
though she had been told to stay?
And if he was very late,
what would she do when she got hungry?
And when it started getting dark?
And what if he never came?
Where would she live?
Who would take care of her?
Would she die?

Perhaps she waited by the flagpole
with all these thoughts until
he at last appeared.

Then, putting them away somewhere,
gave a little wave to him
with a smile that said
she always knew that he would come.

Good Friday

Of all the holy days in the Christian calendar,
this is the most troublesome one for me.
On this day, we are told,
God, the all-powerful party of the first part,
abets the doing in of his innocent son,
the party of the second part,
only to resurrect him from the dead three days later,
so the party of the third part, we,
can be saved from our sins
by the love of the party of the first part.

Hearing this story each year, I cannot help but ask:
how could God get himself into such a predicament?
That the salvation of the world he created
and over which it's said he rules,
should depend on such a terrible sacrifice?

But when I consider all that's come from his creation
of man and woman,
good and evil,
life and death,
quagmire's the word that comes to mind;
and I think perhaps
God felt on that first Good Friday
like Yeltsin must have felt about Chechnya,
or Johnson felt about Vietnam,
or how de Gaulle felt about Algiers,
or maybe how Bush will feel someday about Iraq,
and I see how Good Friday could have been
an act born of desperation.

Then it occurs to me
maybe God isn't like a general at all,
or a head-of-state,
but like an artist.
Maybe he felt like a sculptor
who knows his consciousness—
to create a masterpiece—
must first enter the stone.

Gratitude

Before we four leave,
I check my jacket for the tickets
to Verdi's *Rigoletto*
and give each of the women with me
a gold box of Godiva chocolates
small enough to fit inside a purse.

A man my age should be grateful
to be seen at the opera,
especially this one,
in the company of three beautiful women:
wife, daughter, and girlfriend of his son—
extra grateful.

And should remember
always to be kind,
never make fun,
never be vengeful—
a lesson learned too late
by Verdi's tragic jester.

Haircut

I hate to think how many I've had
in the course of my life,
starting when I was just three or four,
about a month's separation between each one,

maybe a third of them all
gotten right here in this neighborhood shop
a little more than three blocks from my house;
and all of those divided between just two barbers,

one, the owner, by now an old friend,
who will do it all over again today,
and the other who left some years before
to marry a priest—

well, an ex-priest, to be more precise.

I've often wondered if they met here at the shop,
she, scissors in one hand, comb in the other,
deftly working her way around his head,
perhaps trimming his beard,

and he, upright in the chair,
like a man dressed in a poncho,
her thighs brushing ever so lightly
his bare elbow resting inside;

and how she told him one day
she'd often observed
short hair made older men look younger
and younger men look older

which got him to thinking
about what he was doing with his life
and why he was doing it,
and on his way back to the university nearby,

where I'm guessing he taught a course
on Modern Marriage and Family,
he decided the next time he was there,
he would ask her

to cut his hair just a bit shorter.

Halloween Haiku

Yellow light of autumn
Bee crawling on the flower
What does he know?

Low in the sky
The sun going down
Makes long shadows
And turns earth cold.

Full moon rising
Over naked poplars.
In the cornfield,
Rustling leaves.

Souls step softly
Out of endless time
Into the present—
Now it's gone!

From the dying fire
A dream blooming
In the night
Of receding stars.

Happy Birthday

A good night's sleep
Waking up
Next to her
Anna calling
Sweet oatmeal with cream
New vine planting done
Robert there to help
Being back in town today
Morning tea
Rereading poems I wrote this year
A beautiful day to walk
Roses on an old iron fence
One rose in bloom
Coffee at my favorite café table
The noon meeting
Eating lunch outdoors
A card from John and Nancy
Good news from Matthew
Liz and Phil coming home tomorrow
Patrick graduating Saturday
Cooking dinner
Grace's apple pie
Sarah coming in
Dorothy coming over
Presents too
Grandchildren
Nicholas, Annika, Isabel
O's battling Detroit
Another good night's sleep
Ahead.

May 1, 2007

Irina

"Don't falling down,"
said the world figure skating star
from Russia,
when asked her motto.
And falling down
she didn't.
Skating perfectly through her program
of triple lutzes and toe loops,
salchows and camels,
flashing brilliant blade work throughout,
then spinning,
finally unfolding like a flower
into her signature move:
a rear extension of one leg
hand held
high over her head
mirroring the curve of her arched torso,
spinning all the while
on her other leg;
now gliding to her finish,
precisely stopping
when the music stops,
the knowing it was good
emerging on her friendly face
for all to see and being part of.

Italian-American Dinner

For Dorothy

We heard Bill Clinton speak.
I can't remember what he said,
something flattering I'm sure
about the crowd assembled there —
with jokes, of course.

This dinner happens every year;
another big event in a town
where big events are manufactured
like ingots used to be in Pittsburgh.

We were invited by a friend
but my wife proposed
her mother go instead —
which was fine with me.
Proud of her Italian heritage,
I knew she would enjoy being there,
and tell her friends about it later.

My friend seemed disappointed
when I told him who my guest would be;
I'm not sure why he brought his daughter —
perhaps because his wife is Polish.

When he met us in the Hilton lobby
his tone was formal,
his manner almost grave.
I made the introductions;
we said the usual words,

thought we spotted some celebrities,
wondered if the President would show,
and made our way into the ballroom.

He led us to the bar where I'm sure
he expected her to order Pym's Cup
or a sherry, maybe even Dubonnet.
Instead it was a favorite of his own:
gin martini, on-the-rocks,
with a twist.

My friend, surprised, seemed almost happy now.
No problem after all, I suppose he thought—
though he was an olive man himself.

James

was a fast-talking, friendly black man with one arm,
whose work was painting houses—
the stump of his left arm
held the rung of the ladder
while he painted with his right.

Once when doing a job for me,
the fully extended ladder we had
wouldn't let him quite reach
the trim at the peak of the gable.
Wishing to save time and trouble,
I offered to build him a scaffold
three feet above the rest of the yard:

a small, makeshift affair
of some boards on bricks for a base,
two trestles on that,
and some boards on the trestles
would do it I thought.

Eying me for a moment
as if I didn't understand something I should,
he said, *I don't think so.*
And when I asked him why not, he replied,
I don't want folks saying
what a nice guy James was.

Without any further discussion,
he went down to his truck

and drove off to find
the ladder he needed;
but not before turning back with a grin,
and giving a jaunty wave
with his good arm.

July Fourth

It was a good day of work in the garden
before we shower, change, and have some supper,
then move out onto the porch
to do nothing more than see the day depart.

It's a long, second-story porch
lined with white wicker,
open at either end to draw in the cool of evening,
the cool air riding the slight breeze
that stirs the trees in front.
There, the two of us exchange the easy talk
of two people entirely at ease with each other:
talk about the day,
where our children are tonight,
what we want to do tomorrow.
We wonder at the others who sat out here like us
maybe sitting somewhere up there now
nodding their approval or displeasure,
if they care at all.

I can hear the creek not far away;
you hear the rustling in an ancient tree
planted too close to the house
but useful this night
to see a raccoon who lives there
peer out at us between the forking trunk,
then climb further down
and tiptoe out a slender bough,

gradually bending with her weight
until it gently drops her to the ground
where she steps off.

To our surprise
fireworks appear above the trees on a distant hill;
we'd almost forgotten it's the Fourth.
We watch the pyrotechnic worlds
explode into existence and quickly disappear.

After it's over,
I walk the porch's length
to find a darker spot
where I can see the stars.

Away from the light coming from inside
I see the fireflies in the woods
flashing like the cameras at Camden Yards
the night Ripken broke the record
set by Gehrig years before;
thinking the fireflies were flashing that night too
and also the night when real bombs burst in air
above nearby Fort McHenry,
and will still be flashing all the other summer nights
long after Major League Baseball
and Independence Day
are history
and so are we.

Kite

For Sarah

She was a little girl then,
no more than five or six,
wearing that year's Easter dress,
the cotton one with small spring flowers,
the one she liked to twirl in.

You can read in her upturned face
the delight of flying it herself.
Like the life ahead of her,
she holds in her hands
the beginning of a cord
barely visible in the photograph;
and out of camera range,
the long, curved line of cord
we cannot see, pulled by
the unseen wind pushing on
the unseen kite
to which the cord is fastened.

My father, her grandfather,
younger then than I am now,
leans toward her,
arms outstretched,
ready to help if she needs it
but his face confident
she can do it on her own.

Letter from the Shore

I've been here almost a week
and there are so many things I wanted to tell you
I hardly know where to begin.

It rained last night pretty hard
and is still partly cloudy this morning
but the forecast is for clearing later on.

Before breakfast,
I put on our new Murray Perahia recording
of Bach's English Suites,

a performance I can only describe as amazing—
more breathtaking notes in this two CD set
than stars in the Milky Way,

and he still wasn't finished
when I got up to go for a paper
from the box at the end of the street.

I took the ancient Schwinn with fat tires,
the ladies model we bought at the yard sale
with a wicker basket on the handlebars,

and when I left for the news of the day—
of yesterday, really—
I was a man on a mission,

but even with a stop for coffee on the way home,
it was nothing you could call really important,
which I thought apropos for the beach,

especially at this time of year
when the crowds are all gone
and most of the houses are closed for the winter.

The air was cool as I put up the kickstand,
about right for late October along the Delaware coast,
the sun playing hide-and-go seek with the clouds.

So there I am, riding along,
just taking in the ordinary scenery along the way,
nothing on my mind,

just enjoying the morning —
some red and yellow leaves backlit by the sun,
an old man with his dog,

a rabbit scurrying for cover into the reeds,
a box turtle nervously crossing the road,
the morning light reflected off the wetland tidepools.

I'm thinking as I ride on, it's all so simple,
why can't it be like this every day?
Is there anything I could be doing better than this?

When I finally get to the shop,
the woman behind the counter calls me "Hon,"
as in short for Honey, as she hands me my coffee,

as if she's known me for years,
an overly familiar manner I find somewhat annoying,
but pass off as just a part of American culture,

having run into the practice in Boston
as well as the Bronx,
Baton Rouge, and Biloxi.

On the way out of the shop,
I pass an oldish man—a ringer for Alexander
Solzhenitsyn—with his book open to a chapter

I can see is labeled "Leading a Purposeful Life,"
and I see too there is a bulletized list of what follows
like in a *Retirement for Dummies*

(if there is such a thing),
although I can't quite make out
what the list says.

I wonder if maybe he's a writer
who's had enough, perhaps, of writing,
and wants to turn a page,

but he strikes me by his looks
as someone more likely to be
an engineer recently retired from NASA,

someone who's having trouble
making the transition from one phase of his life
to the next and knows he needs help.

Anyway, when I get home,
Murray is still at it but after so many notes
I feel he can't have far to go,

and his playing is so brilliant
and, the music, well, so purposeful,
it almost makes me feel guilty

how little I have to show
that matters to anyone
on a day such as this

and whether even this letter counts for anything
when, just like that, Solzhenitsyn, rimless glasses, beard,
and all, pops back in my mind

which reminds me of the anonymous message
I saw earlier scratched on the top of the table
next to my coffee: "I love Lindsey,"

and I think of the messenger who wrote it
for whom Lindsey at that moment was purpose enough,
and then I think of you

and how, from the very beginning
it's always been enough
for me too.

So until you get here,
all my love,
W.

Liebestod

[handwritten: One of my favorite Waynian pieces.]

A single cell divides
making two new cells
identical to the original.
For mitosis, that is all there is
to reproduction.

[handwritten: of stuff Mitosis no no war.]

Meiosis on the other hand
is just the opposite:
two cells of similar origin fuse
creating one new cell,
different from the other two,
but much like the bodies that produced it,
bodies which the new cell leaves behind.

[handwritten: do say the cause of all evil.]

There is nothing left behind in mitosis,
no remainder drops away, then dies;
from that there is no parting.
There is no endless darkness;
there are no ghosts;
and there appears to be
no love either.

Life Force

What makes the engine go?
Stanley Kunitz

We often have to laugh when caught by it,
unawares, under the covers,
after a long day,
taking comfort in a spoon,
anticipating nothing more than sleep;

what Cole Porter famously observed
was the universal tendency
of all who came by twos into the Ark;
more or less what
the companions of my wasted youth
were searching for when they so unartfully described
kissing as upper persuasion for lower invasion;
or what leads Dorabella and Fiordiligi
to inconstancy in Mozart's *Cosi;*
the desire "that makes us wretched,"
according to da Ponte.

Cole's song equated doing it with falling in love.
I'm not sure it's the same as
the love John Lennon said was all we need
or what Wagner had in mind
when Tristan and Isolde die in each other's arms —
but maybe it is.

I first heard the term years ago
in G. B. Shaw's play *Man and Superman,*
in a theatre close to campus,

not far from Harvard Square.
Young and newly married,
I had no trouble seeing what it was
Don Juan was getting at.

And it's just as clear to me today.
But whether you call it the life force
love, lust, or something else,
always and everywhere
we keep coming back for more —
finite players in an infinite game.

Love

It's 6:03 in the morning when I get up to use the
bathroom and 6:06 when I crawl back in bed, pull up the
still warm covers and think how good it feels to be here
with her—*good*, the unexpected one-word answer from
our granddaughter, Isabel, who'd just turned three, to
her mother's question, *What do you say?* after opening
three of our five birthday presents without a word or
even a pause between each one; and at 6:30, the radio
comes on and I hear Garrison Keillor say, *It's Friday,
October 27, 2006, and it's the birthday of Dylan Thomas born
in Seaswan, Wales in 1914; and it's the birthday of Sylvia
Plath born in Boston, Massachusetts in 1932,* and nothing
more about either of these dead greats; but instead goes
on at length about Zadie Smith, a writer I barely heard
of, also born this day, who grew up in a working class,
London neighborhood in a *housing project that was half
English and half Irish, . . .a black family squished between two
tribes at war,* he quotes her as saying, which I think is
pretty good; and her college experience as *people reading
books in a posh place,* also good, but thinking her
confession about how much she is influenced by what
she reads—*I think if I carry on plagiarizing for 15 years, it
will settle like silt, and I'll write something really great,* is
really good; wishing afterward while hearing in the
background it's going to be cloudy and cold this
morning with rain in the afternoon that he'd said more
about Dylan Thomas and thinking fondly of the last lines
of *A Child's Christmas in Wales,* and how good they are,
especially *the music rising up the long, steadily falling night,*
and how I shared Keillor's feeling about Plath which I'd

heard him hold forth on once though can't recall now
where; and hearing Plath's name makes me think of Ted
Hughes and I wonder what he'd be doing today, her
birthday, were he still alive, and then of *Richard* Hughes
and how I used some lines of his from *High Wind in
Jamaica* as the frontispiece for something I'd written
years ago which I still remember: *Of course it is not really
so cut and dried as all this; but often the only way of
attempting to express the truth is to build it up, like a card
house, of a pack of lies,* and thinking that was *damn* good;
and later getting up and going down to find Naguib
Mafouz's *Palace of Desire,* the second volume of his Cairo
Trilogy all three of which I am extremely fond of, and
the lines at the end where Kamal is talking to himself
about death; and I read, *Belief in God makes death a
bewildering but wise decree, when actually it's nothing but a
cruel joke,* and Yasin tells him, *This is the way the world is.
You must come to know it as it really is,* thinking how good
that is and remembering Mafouz also died this year, then
somehow thinking of the poem of Carruth's I was
reading yesterday, especially the lines, *It's a high wind
now . . . Hear it rising, then breaking, then rising again, and
breaking again . . . this is the gathering of our love into all
love, into that suffering and joy,* which I think is very, very
good although I wouldn't have said it quite that way,
but rather:

*Love is the gathering of our life and death
into all life and death,
into that good we cannot know,
cannot reach, cannot express,
yet believe is.*

More Haiku

not bad

Awakened by the rain,
a noisy torrent
rushes past my window.

I turn away
but through closed shutters,
the morning light slips in my room.

Hunted rabbit;
down the gun barrel,
we stare into each other's eyes.

Snow falls through the night.
In the early morning,
I can hear the silence.

Fresh cut grass, bread baking,
sea breeze, land breeze,
no mistaking what they are.

Nice

For John

is nice, they say,
the beautiful city on the French Riviera;
neither of us had been there before,
but we had a plan we thought would work.

We met in Paris, a slight detour for him,
on his way to England to play golf,
and me, there, in the City of Light
to attend a conference on spent nuclear fuel.

Not auspicious circumstances perhaps,
for a trip to Provence,
but it was something we wanted to do—
not sure when such an occasion would happen again,
and so far it hasn't and probably won't.

As soon as conditions allowed,
we boarded the TGV at le Gare de Lyon,
headed southeast to Dijon,
then due south to Lyon,
the French countryside flying by
at 500 kilometers per hour;
down the Rhone Valley,
skirting the Massif Central,
then left along the Cote d'Azur
after gliding into Marseille,
and we were there.

The hotel was fine and in the late afternoon,
we started walking Old Nice:
down the Promenade des Anglais,
past the Negresco Hotel, the Casino Ruhl,
and along the Quai des Etats-Unis.

During the two days we were there,
we toured the sights like anyone else;
saw Le Chateau on a bluff overlooking the town,
Bellanda Tour where Berlioz composed,
the port of Lympia where Garibaldi was born,
and the churches, of course; in addition
to strolling the city itself, plus sunbathing
on the pebbly beach by the sea.

The day before we were planning to leave,
we rented a car so we could drive
to the border that evening,
cross into Italy for dinner,
and stop in Monaco on the way back;
then return to Paris the following day
spending one night on the road —
which we did.

We left Nice that last afternoon;
it was nice being together again.
Once our roads were congruent
but now they'd diverged
and soon he'd return to the road he was on
and I'd do the same.

But for a moment, there we were,
just the two of us,
father and son,
high above the sea,
driving through the hills of Provence,
down the road that leads to San Remo.

Nice.

Night Walk

"Where are you going?"
he heard her call
but didn't answer
except to slam the door.

He walked along the sidewalk
against the traffic
but at this hour
there was none—
only the oncoming headlights
of an occasional car.

Hunched over against the cold,
the weight of anger
he thought would sink him had he stayed
began to lift
as he strode through street after street
of darkened houses,
until the burden of his wrath was gone.

He began to think of her,
of all the pleasures they had had;
of a summer day when they first were lovers
when he stood behind her almost touching,
while craning to see over a wall
on a street he'd been down
earlier this night.

It was then he turned for home.
He slid his key into the lock,
felt the tumblers move into position
before he turned the key to throw the bolt.

He went upstairs,
slipped off his clothes and slid between the covers,
entering the warmth coming toward him
though she was turned away.

Wordless, he lay,
finally at rest, at peace,
content to lie there next to her
as if he didn't know
he would stay forever,
and fell asleep as the morning sun
filled the room with light.

October 1

It was a Valentine's Day present for my wife.
Two years ago they sold it off the wall to me,
having a cup of coffee in the café where it hung,
thinking that morning about what to get for her.

A photograph of a sculpture by Brancusi,
The Kiss: two stone figures locked
in a permanent embrace, standing,
toe-to-toe, eyes closed, each with their arms
around the shoulders of the other,
oblivious to me, the girl behind the counter,
the old man sitting at a table by the window,
to everything but each other;
solid figures, barely carved, almost alike,
their genders barely discernable.

She sat it on the bookshelf
with the photographs of our children
and our grandchildren
where it sits today, our anniversary,
and reminds me of the time
when first we felt the power
Brancusi's art is reaching for
that fastens us together still,
having the same need for the other,
greater than any other need.

Off-season Trip

It's early but we are eager to leave.
We lock up the house in town,
put the few things we are taking
in the back of the car
and head east for our house at the beach.
Only a few people are out at this hour
and once we cross Chesapeake Bay Bridge
we have the road to ourselves.

A layer of morning fog, like a shroud,
drapes over the dead fields of the Eastern Shore.
The day is clear except for the fog
refracting the winter sunlight for miles
along the road over the flat coastal plain.
Salisbury Public Radio plays Vivaldi and Bach
plus some Rachmaninoff—
Rhapsody on a Theme by Paganini—
not exactly our idea of morning music
but we've noticed over the years
Sergey's a favorite of theirs.

Denton, Bridgeville, Millsboro—
we take turns driving
but the two of us know the way so well
the car almost drives itself.
We make our usual stops for coffee
and to stretch our legs.

Once there, we'll light a fire, read and cook,
drive the deserted streets of our ghost town,

walk the boardwalk with a few other hardy souls;
we'll stop in the bookstore (open all winter),
enjoy the big sky, the long line,
the tidal wetlands behind our house;
in the evening, do some cooking,
or maybe go out for a pizza.

Now we are almost there.
We sing some songs,
one of our oldest connections:
all the words to all the songs we both know.
"Oh we ain't got a barrel of money,
"Maybe we're ragged and funny..."

We turn into our street.
We see a few others also have come
and then we are home.
Trip over, we step out
to breathe the air.

Ah, the air!

Other Plans

He was the youngest of our six children, the last one to
do each of the things his older brothers and sisters had
already done, including how to ride a bike with only two
wheels. We had worked at it off and on during that long
summer day, back-and-forth on the flat, dead-end street
in front of our house at the beach, him wanting to learn,
unsteady at first, but gradually getting the feel of it and
me running beside him, reaching out to balance him
when he started to fall. Just before going in for dinner,
he was doing so well I let him go on his own, a decision I
was soon sorry for when he lost his balance near the end
of the street and I wasn't there to catch him before he
crashed, skinning his knee on the gravel to boot. I
helped him get up and tried to assure him his spill was a
fluke but I knew how it hurt and what had been done to
his pride. I urged him to give it another try right then
and there like they say you should do if you're thrown
from a horse, but he wasn't having any of that so we
called it quits for the day. The next morning at breakfast
I down-played the fall, reminded him of how well he
had done and how far he had gone on his own, and then
made a pitch for picking up where we had stopped. He
said no, he wasn't going to ride his bike that day and
when I asked him why not, he announced he had other
plans. Just like that: "I have other plans," he said, as if
no other explanation was needed. Of course I had

encountered this strain of, shall we say, independence in all of our kids but I was taken aback nevertheless—he was only five after all—and marveled how alike they all were despite their difference in age.

Pillow Talk

Pillow Talk was not one of Pauline Kael's
5001 Nights at the Movies
even though it won an Oscar
the year I turned twenty-one.
I thought I remembered liking it
way back when,
but last night on TV
the romantic possibilities
of Rock Hudson and Doris Day
sharing a two-party phone line
now seemed quainter than Hammerstein's
surrey with the fringe on top
and not as clever or as titillating
as once I'd thought.

If I was making a movie about pillow talk,
real pillow talk, not the Hollywood version,
there would be a couple, in bed, in the dark,
one facing the ceiling,
the other turned away,
nothing but anger filling the space between them,
thinking their own thoughts,
each determined this time it will be different.

Then maybe wishing
they hadn't gone quite so far
or said it quite that way,
maybe wishing nothing had been said at all.
Not sure whether they should let it go tonight
and take it up again tomorrow,

or hoping to get past it altogether
without another word;
but knowing too that wouldn't work.
Not even sure now who's at fault
or if it really matters anyway.

Finally one or the other speaks;
two or three words is all it takes
to span the chasm.
Each knows the reaching out,
like the bridge Alec Guiness built,
won't last for long;
the war is still going on
but they make the effort anyway.

As the sun begins to penetrate the darkness,
the camera sees the sleeping pair,
all peaceful now,
nestled in the morning light.

In my movie,
the next scene would be much like the last.
I'm not quite sure how it ends—
or if it ever does.

Pitching

It wasn't
a bad pitch:
plenty of heat,
good movement,
but at that point
in the count
a bad decision:
hitter looking
fast ball to drive.
Too late now.
Gave him
the high hard one
and drive it he did
over the left field wall,
trotting the bases
after rounding first.
Should have given him
the slider.

Playoffs

Now the Mets are down
three games to two in the NLCS
and the Cardinals are celebrating tonight
victory in St. Louis
before flying off to Flushing in New York
to try and seal the deal at Shea
where the Mets are said to have home field advantage
which they will sorely need to win two straight
and advance to the World Series
and take on the Tigers from Detroit.

All year long the announcers tell us
what it's all about:
for *quality* pitching,
it's trusting your stuff
and release point,
arm angle, command,
and mixing up your pitches,
coming in on the batter
and staying away,
changing speeds,
staying down in the zone
and not overthrowing.

Hitting, on the other hand, they say,
is all about a short and compact swing,
plate coverage and power—
but not just power,
not just the long ball—
but also going to the opposite field,

159

hitting it where they ain't,
having a good eye,
not trying to do too much,
knowing how to bunt,
and how to execute the hit and run.

Defense is all about keeping them off the board,
not letting them get on base
or if they do not letting them advance,
otherwise known as making outs.
Offense is all about getting runners on,
getting them over
and getting them home, i.e.,
if it isn't obvious,
scoring runs.

Sometimes it gets very rarified,
like Joe Morgan telling Jon Miller
just the other night
it's all about letting the game
breathe.

And let's not forget the cynics
who say it's all about the money,
and when you hear what the players make,
buy a hot dog at the park,
a Bud or Miller Lite,
sit through 162 regular games of advertising on TV,
then the playoffs and the Series too,
it's easy to agree with them.

The fans?
Well, that's a different story.

We know it's all about suffering and joy:
the agony of defeat;
how sweet it is to win.
This year we're rooting for the Mets
our daughter's boyfriend's favorite team,
and also because her mother's from Forest Hills, NY
(and so is her grandmother
and so was her grandfather who is dead now
but was a Mets fan after the Giants moved to
San Francisco.)

As I was saying,
her mother lived in Forest Hills,
which isn't far from Shea;
also it's the Mets we're rooting for
because the Nats came to Washington
from Montreal in '05
and are also in the National League
in the same Division (East) as the Mets.
Of course, we're also rooting for Detroit
since I'm from Baltimore and we've rooted for the O's
more years than I care to admit,
through mostly losing seasons,
and almost never in the playoffs,
whose League is the American
which Detroit is also in.
(This would be a different story
had the Yankees won and not the Tigers.)

So that is where it stands for now.
It's easy (even reassuring in these times)
to see when you step back and look at baseball
why it's called our National Pastime—

the hours alone required to follow a whole season
would make it so;
why we say baseball is as American as apple pie,
since it's a simple sport that anyone can play—
although having helped my wife
make many more than one,
I have to wonder if there isn't
more to pie.

[Note: In 2006, the Cardinals went on to take the NLCS in
seven games, then beat the Tigers in the World Series, four
games to one.]

Punt Return

For Patrick

Brian Mitchell
(still the NFL leader in return yards gained),
suits up a little different now,
doing Redskin's post-game for Comcast SportsNet
with two other guys.

But this was way back when
in the mid-'90's of the previous century
at the Coleman Power Sports showroom,
the Skin's new star running back at the door
offering 8"x 10" glossies of himself, autographed,
to any and all coming in;
a clean-cut, well-built, cheerful young man,
at 5' 10" and 220 pounds, powerful,
but not nearly as big as I thought he would be.

The older of my two youngest sons
accepted the photo without missing a beat—
where it is now I haven't a clue.
But his brother balked, then refused.
"Baseball's more my game," he said,
to the obvious surprise of the star.

Sometimes in a game,
this football great had to retreat
for a punt with good hang-time
and far deeper than he thought it would be.
When he did, he could signal fair-catch
with a wave of his hand

and go to the sidelines
instead of returning the ball;
but that was not his M.O.

And this was no different.

"That's smart," he said to my son.
"If you're good, the money is better,
"And you get to play twice as long."

Not a bad return, I thought;
like a speedy scamper up-field,
several good moves,
breaking a tackle or two,

but brought down short of the goal line
by the kid who punted the ball.

Quantum Physics

In *Six Easy Pieces*, the book,
not to be confused with *Five Easy Pieces*,
the movie,
Feynman says, "Yes, Physics has given up."
In the world of the atom
only the chance that something will happen
is all we can predict,
we cannot *know* more than that.

Though Feynman is at pains to stress
things on atomic scale behave
like nothing that we know of,
for someone who's raised six children
(not six easy pieces I can assure you)
the uncertainty principle,
while not exactly humdrum,
is certainly not a new idea.

Doing the math, though
on all the decisions they make,
large and small,
that's another matter altogether.
Will they choose for good?
Or ill?
Who knows?

It makes you empathize with Einstein
who never did give up on
explaining everything with certainty,

165

a concept of reality not much indulged in
today, at least by physicists;
(though still popular with most politicians
and some pundits.)

But real life, as every parent knows,
imitates not only art,
but quantum physics too.

Rainmaker

Meditating this morning on this Quaker claim, the
thought that came to mind was of Lizzie Curry, H.C.'s
daughter in N. Richard Nash's play, *The Rainmaker*,
which we saw at Washington's Arena Stage not too long
ago with two old friends, a play set in the drought-
stricken West during the Great Depression where,
according to the playbill which luckily I saved and now
am reading, it hasn't rained for so long it seems that rain
will never come again, or will be too late to save the
Curry family from ruin when it does, a time when men
of wisdom like H.C. Curry "know how to be patient with
heaven," in Nash's words but young people like Lizzie
don't, perhaps because she fears her spirit, like the earth
around her, might be dying also, believing as she does
that she is plain and will never find a man to love her
and to love, a man like Deputy Sheriff File, a man she's
had her eyes on but who's rebuffed her modest ploys to
lure him in, a man determined to never trust a woman
with his heart again, a man who says he is a widower
but everyone knows is just a story he's invented to cover
up the blow to his pride when his wife left him—for a
school teacher.

And that's the playbill's summary of the plot when Bill
Starbuck happens on the scene, the charismatic
rainmaker of the title, a rain priest promising them
deliverance—for a price of course—and although

H.C.'s family can't agree, H.C. signs on anyway and the family settles down to watch and wait to see what he can do, not sure if he is just a con-man, a trickster on the make and on the move or something more, and they are still in doubt at the end even though it rains, since before it does, he and Lizzie fall in love and each begins to trust the other and themselves in ways they haven't done before, and when they end up in each other's arms, H.C. realizes there may be more to Starbuck than he bargained for especially when it looks like Lizzie might run off with him, but before she can the climax comes when File asks her not to, a humble plea he couldn't bring himself to make when his wife was walking out on him, so that now, like a cloudburst, Lizzie goes from having no man to two and she has to ask herself will it be File or Starbuck, the Sheriff or the shaman?

And at the end, when she chooses drab Sheriff File not the flamboyant magician Starbuck, after all that's happened, we have to wonder why. What is it Nash is telling us? Sometimes we have to take a chance to go on living?—Yes. For Lizzie, it's taking a chance on love, first on Starbuck, then on File. But for her drought-stricken spirit, before the curtain closes, Lizzie chooses love for someone she thinks more like herself, someone not so different, someone more her equal. Maybe Nash is saying that's the way to play it safe in love. And suddenly I'm struck by the thought that the message in the Quaker line is there is no such difference and there is no such safety. But I think I would have missed it had she gone the other way.

Rocky

He always said America
was the greatest country in the world,
and he told me once,
when he and his brother got off the plane from Iran—
thirty years ago now—
they kissed the ground at Logan Airport.
Really. Not figuratively.

He wasn't built like Sylvester Stallone,
but at 5'6" and 135 pounds,
he was surely as strong if not stronger;
Rocky, short for Harak,
former self-styled camel driver,
now sole proprietor of his own business,
a hauler of trash.

God knows how much he has hauled;
when I think of all the old studs, joists, floorboards,
plaster and laths he's hauled just for me,
it's like a small mountain.

You can do whatever you want here, he said,
as long as you obey the law.

The U.S. of A. was the magic kingdom for him,
and I'm guessing the source of his pride
was more about gratitude
than anything else.

As for my electrician and plumber,
I'm not quite so sure;
when I called them last winter
for a job I was doing,
one was vacationing in Bermuda,
and the other was spending two weeks in Cancun.

Second Grade

Twenty strong plus their teacher,
the second grade arrives in single file
for early morning mass.
Girls in blouses and blue plaid skirts,
boys in khaki pants and blue knit shirts,
standard issue socks and shoes.
They take the four long benches
behind the row I'm in.
They stand when we stand,
sit when we sit,
kneel when we kneel,
say what we say —
the girls more uniformly than the boys.
Too young to receive communion
like the rest of us,
instead they line up after we are served,
arms across their chests
to receive, one-by-one,
a blessing from the priest.
After mass,
they file out the double doors,
happy that it's over.

Twenty years ago and more,
offspring of my own
were coming through those doors
with their class.
I was far away
doing my work, of course,
as they were doing theirs.

Today, others are where I was then
and I am where they'll wish they'd been
twenty years from now
when they like me
will wonder why they weren't.

Solstice

Death is like the shadow of geraniums
blooming by the window
bathed in winter light.
We want to believe our souls
are like the flower's glory,
an aura of transcendent power,
beautiful and fair,
at one with destiny.
Otherwise, it's life, then
only death.
But sometimes we can't believe.

Sunflowers

Early in his career,
Puccini wrote a piece for strings,
Chrysanthemums,
intended, I suppose, to be
a musical interpretation of the flower,
the sound of the flower, if you will,
for him.

Today at the market
shopping with my wife,
we bought some sunflowers,
one of her favorites,
to celebrate something of a windfall
she'd received at work.
When we got home, I noticed
the sunflower was like
the illustrations of sound
you often see in comics or cartoons:
lines radiating from a radio or whatever source;
here, it was the yellow petals of sound
surrounding the dark brown seed-head of a speaker,
a flower of sound rather than,
like Puccini,
the sound of a flower.

The Clearing

It had rained for two days,
a hard rain,
after a long, hot month
of late-summer drought.
But on the day of the wedding
planned for outdoors,
the weather cleared behind a front of cool air
moving east over the mountains.

So under a blue sky and great cumulus clouds,
we heard again the reading
from First Corinthians, Chapter 13,
telling us the true meaning of love,
and its place,
above both faith and hope,
and we heard the vows taken,
down by the waterfall.

Then we drove up the steep grade
to the house where the reception would be,
to a high mountain clearing,
where tents had been raised,
and RV's and campers of overnight guests
were parked off to the sides
like a makeshift circle of wagons
protecting the safety of those
inside its perimeter.
And after the food was served
but before the wine overflowed,
and before everyone settled in folding chairs

to enjoy the rest of the day,
and before the cake had been cut,
and long before the kids had gone off
to play games of their own,
the four-piece band began to warm up
with a couple of tunes everyone knew,
and then the woman on keyboard announced
they would do one for the newly wed couple,
one to which they were invited to dance.

She was a contralto
with a voice like the mythical sirens,
and when she started to sing
a slow love-song by a modern St. Paul,
the guests became quiet
and turned their attention
to the couple dancing on grass
under the awning,
one in lace, one in leather,
each in the arms of the other.

I thought the minds of everyone there
cleared for a moment,
remembering the times
they too had danced.

The couple finished their dance.
The party went on
and by evening,
the party was over.
Not many days after,
the high mountain clearing
was filling with snow.

Umbrella

A shutter
is like an eyelid,
it must be closed
to do its work.

An umbrella
is like the heart,
useless when it rains
unless it's open.

Valentines

THE WILL TO WIN
IS NOTHING

is what I read on the rear of his tee,
all that was showing above the café chair
holding his coat—
that, and the back of his head.

It was a sentiment I could agree with
but somehow seemed too wise for this boy and girl,
he in his tee and she in her tank-top and jeans
with her carelessly falling, shoulder-length hair,

sitting across the table from him facing us both.
She looked at him squarely all of the time,
a beautiful face, especially the eyes,
like Callas must have looked at twenty or so,

as if she was looking for something
she hadn't found yet.
She didn't talk much except to respond
to what he was saying,

sometimes asking a question or two,
a flicker of smile spaced here and there;
interested but subject to change,
friendly but short of approval,

even perhaps, as the tee shirt advised,
indifferent to winning;
but all perfectly natural like taking a walk
or getting dressed in the morning.

Just when I thought they both
may be taking the words too much to heart,
he leaned across the table and kissed her,
nothing overdone, just a kiss

which she accepted calmly,
not surprised but rather I'd say, prepared for,
and I think happily,
since she smiled a look back at him

I hadn't seen before.
And then he kissed her again.
When they got up to leave,
the last lines of his tee came into view.

It was then I read
what I guessed
they both knew all along—
the will to win is nothing

WITHOUT THE WILL
TO PREPARE

Who's Afraid of Virginia Woolf?

Appropriate,
given the state of our Union,
that this year's Edward Albee Festival
at Washington's Arena Stage
should begin with this one,
arguably his best,
a bitter vintage:
the venomous Martha,
the violent George,
the unwitting Nick and Honey,
the disastrous late-night after-party
fueled by endless alcohol,
proving marriage
sometimes works in cruel ways,
almost like war,
defying reason.

Yes, certainly that
is one thing Albee is telling us,
but maybe also this:
knowing life as it really is —
that life goes on but we do not,
that only love makes our life worthwhile,
but love won't save us in the end —
makes us very angry,
vengeful;
makes us want to hurt,
to savage and abuse love,
even reject love
to spite the misery of death,

makes us want to act out our rage
toward such an inexplicable creation,
where love and death
are seemingly endowed
with such unequal powers.

This mystery stew of love and death,
so skewed toward death,
could make Albee's characters
want to play some vicious games
like *Humiliate the Host* in Act I,
Get the Guests or
Hump the Hostess in Act II,
and even resort to *Bringing Up
Baby* in Act III, that taboo topic
flanked by love and death.

Who's afraid of living life
without the illusion love will save us?

In the last lines of his play,
Martha could be quietly confessing she is.

And on whom shall our terrible,
fear-bred anger be unleashed?

Who else is there, answers Albee,
but each other?

Writing Poetry

is like fishing (for me):
first, you get your gear together—
that's taking my cup of tea
up to the library after breakfast
and getting out my notebook;

then you head out to the stream
and find a likely-looking spot—
that's adjusting the shutters for the light
and settling into my chair;

then you take out your rod, attach a lure to the line,
and wade into the water, ready to begin—
that's looking at my notes from the day before
and reconnecting with the muse;

you cast a line toward a likely looking place—
that's finding something
I thought had promise for a poem,
something I'd read or heard or seen,
or just popped into my head.

You wait.
When nothing happens, you pull in the line
and cast it out again
and keep doing it until something does—
for me, the hardest work of poetry:
feeling there is something there,
not knowing what it is,
or yet how to say it.

Then if you're lucky, a big one strikes
and you pull the line to set the hook—
that's getting the idea, the title and the first lines right;

then comes the reeling in,
sometimes letting out some line,
sometimes moving around the stream
to get a better angle—
that's writing down everything that comes to mind
often rewriting as I go,
crossing out, and going at it another way.

You can't tell how long it will take to land a fish;
sometimes they put up a fight, sometimes they don't,
sometimes they are clever at avoiding being caught,
sometimes they aren't—
that's the pleasure of the work:
playing with a line, sometimes just a word or two,
sometimes just a comma.

But at last you have him in the water
there in front of you;
you ease him closer and land him with the net—
that's when each new draft
has fewer and fewer changes;
until at last I find I'm going back to words
I used in other versions—
and that is when I stop.

Sometimes of course, they get away
and you come home with an empty creel—
that's when my wife comes home from work,
asks what kind of day I had
and I have to tell her.

Xanadu

Of Xanadu in *Kubla Khan,*
A vision in a dream,
Coleridge once said,
on waking he tried to reconstruct
all that he had seen,
but after writing fifty lines
he mostly tried in vain.
Everyone has woken with
the vivid memory of a dream
only to discover not long after
the dream was gone
except some fragments
we still clung to—
like our lives:
each day like some lines of *Kubla Khan,*
and all our days, like Xanadu.

Yellow Bicycle

For Elizabeth

She was so determined
that summer, all of ten, to get the bike,
the neon yellow one with chrome trim
and brilliant spoke reflectors.
The one she'd seen—
I can't remember where.

She worked every day
selling lemonade
until she had enough
to pay for it,
adjusting her location
to maximize her sales,
working on her pitch
to make it irresistible.

We were surprised
how little time it took
to reach her goal
once she figured out the spot
where they got off the bus was best
and told them what
she was working for.
"How can they say 'No,'" she said,
"to a little girl selling lemonade
"to buy a bike she wants?"

For sure, she loved that yellow bike
but I always thought she loved
the getting of it
just as much
or maybe even more.

She's had some other yellow bikes since then
but they are nothing new for her:
first the goal, next the plan,
and once the wheels are turning,
the brilliant spoke reflectors
flashing in the light.

Zag

is what I should have done
rather than what I did —
which was zig.
Life's most persistent questions
turn out to be not what it means
but what you do:
hold or fold,
stay or go,
fight or flight,
yes or no.

Looking back,
it seems clear now
I often went one way
when I should have gone the other
and worse,
I didn't learn from my mistakes
but kept insisting
if a coin turned up heads once
it would turn up heads once more
when flipped again.

It's a relief these choices
seem to come with less frequency
now — for me,
but not so for my children
or their children,

out there
zigging and zagging like mad,
and like me,
definitely zigging
I'm convinced,
more often than zagging.

III.

A Photograph

There I am
that summer,
on one knee
in the pasture,
bare-shouldered
in my bib-overalls,
bare feet,
and wide-brimmed
straw hat,
hardly more
than six;
and behind me,
two cows,
Spot and Strawberry,
grazing near the stream.

Seeing him now
in a photograph
so many years later,
I can't remember
how it was then
being him.
Though once
I knew him well
and cared for him,

I feel about him today,
perhaps like
my guardian angel
will feel about me
someday,
in the afterlife.

Afternoon

On the wall behind the sofa
hang four large scenes of Rome,
black impressions on creamy paper
from engravings made by Piranesi,

facing Emile Gruppe''s oil,
the *Hammond Schooner*,
in early morning grays,
sails furled,

all hands below,
at anchor in the harbor
of a small New England town,
across the room.

As a boy,
I traveled that coast once
with my parents,
and not so long ago

ate lunch in that piazza,
climbed the Spanish steps,
paused by the famous fountain,
photographed the Campidoglio.

Soon the sun that fills this room with light
will drop from view,
pulling the light away;
the Eternal City will dim,

the coast will fade,
and as night falls,
leave a room filled only with darkness,
or so it will seem.

Apocalypse

This is the end,
the last Act,
the sum of it all,
ground zero.

This is the inflection point—
what once held the water in
now spills the water out.

Like a river going over a falls
descending through the air
is torn apart by some unseen force,
so too the river of our common good
now divides into many separate waters,
all somehow free of their hold
on one another,

and this time
there will be no recovery,
this time will be different:
no rushing water coming together again
in a quiet pool further down the river bed,
no more the ancient, meandering march
to the open sea.

Birds and Bees

A bee
landed in the pool
then fought in vain
to free himself.
I scooped him out
before he drowned,
tired,
too wet at first to fly.
On the paving stones
he sun-dried himself
almost enough
to fly again, when
suddenly a bird
swooped down,
plucked him up,
and carried him
away.

Blue Heron

Late afternoon;
the day was almost done.
As I walked the winding road,
around a bend
I saw a blue heron
fishing in the meadow creek for minnows.
A long way from tide or marsh,
at the far inland edge of his natural range,
I had seen him only once or twice before.
Unconcerned for me
or on either bank the grazing cows,
the great bird gathered himself,
stretching like a ballerina on her toes,
and slowly beat his broad wings.
Then, rising heavenward in the summer air
and tucking in his head and horny legs and feet,
he took flight,
soared above the treetops—
and was gone.

Bruegel

In the dark above my bed,
like a dream of Chagall,
I am floating over
a long-forgotten village—
the village of Pieter Bruegel
not the village of Vitebsk—
a village now buried by the silt of time
but then alive with people:
a woman scrubbing windows from a ladder,
another drawing water from a well,
some women cleaning fish,
a man collaring a wayward child,
another peeing on a wall,
others arguing,
two children spinning tops,
a boy waving a flag
of orange, red, and white.
There is something greater
than each person here
and yet a something to which
each gives meaning,
in the village together,
in the late medieval light,
before night fell,
and they went inside.

Change

Disappointment
I could understand
but I thought it odd for him,
my oldest friend,
to assume he could correct the world
when it wasn't giving him his way,
to be angry when he couldn't keep things
as they were (or as he thought they'd been),
when we both knew our time had passed,
that only the illusions of our age remained
and the disguises we put on
to recreate the world we thought we loved.

Coincidence

As a remarkable occurrence,
it wasn't so much—
earlier that day,
a friend,
down on his luck,
stopped by my table
and asked to borrow $10.

When I took out my wallet,
all I had was four singles
which I was happy to give him
and he was glad to receive.

Walking home from the café,
I was admiring
the stick-figure drawing in chalk
on the sidewalk—
a child's smiling self-portrait
hand-in-hand with her mother—

when I saw the two bills
lying together,
a five and a one,
the five folded in quarters,
the one roughly rolled up.

Finding no rightful owner nearby,
I picked them both up,
put the bills in my pocket,

and promised myself
to pass them along to my friend
the next time I saw him.

I thought it was curious
it happened that way
but would have been
even more strange
for him and for me
had I found them
on the way there.

Credo

Ham-sa.
I am that.
Buddhist mantra

It seems like a simple idea to me
that there is one world
and everything is part of it;

that each part forms
an integral element of the whole,
even what appears to be
orthogonal or even opposite;

that everything derives
from a singular beginning—
wisteria blossoms
and weeping willows
are supported from above
by the seed
of a single starting point below.

Like binary stars
revolving around each other
held together
by their mutual gravitation,
all is pendent,
as the poet Saigyo says,
not independent.

Dark Angel

Sitting on an old log,
part of a locust tree
felled years ago
and cut into lengths
to be split into posts,

I pick off a piece of loose bark
the size of my hand
and see the alarmed ants
racing for safety in every direction,
like an explosion
ignited by fear;

like I'm the Dark Angel,
the Dark Angel looking for them.

And I want to say, *No, no,*
I am not the Dark Angel;
though I may appear otherwise,
we share the same fate.

But the ants learned long ago
about the danger of waiting for answers,
and are gone from my sight in an instant;

only the legless, white grubs
who will die if not fed by the ants —
if not eaten first by the birds —,
and only the tree,
left behind.

Downed Branch

This morning on my usual walk
I passed a downed branch from a ginkgo tree,
a casualty of the storm the night before;
a troublesome branch for traffic
had it fallen in the street,
but harmless on the sidewalk where it landed,
disconnected from all it had been part of.
The fan-shaped leaves seemed as vital
as those on unbroken boughs,
as if unaware of their new reality,
as if still possessed of being alive
though irreversibly cut off from the living,
like those who've died
we sometimes see again
in dreams soon after.

Dynamic Braking

. . .a single short poem has room for history, music, psychology, religious thought, mood, occult speculation, character, and events of one's life.

Robert Bly

Well, he doesn't mention science or technology so unless you assume such subjects come under the heading of occult speculation, which I doubt that they do, I don't know whether this one on electrical engineering and physics is really a poem at all or if maybe the key word is "short" and long poems are different although I've written what I thought were a few short poems where there are at least references to physics and maybe a couple where I thought physics was definitely the subject but now I'm not sure they are poems and if not, just what they are.

So read on at your own risk and if you are ready I would like to begin, although why I start this poem in prose with my first appearance on stage, that and the recollection of a storybook from early childhood, well, maybe I'll figure it out at the end but right now it's a mystery to me though somehow seemed right when I got the idea at a table in my favorite bookshop while reading a copy of Tony Hoagland's poems, *donkey gospel*, which for the record doesn't have a single poem about either physics or engineering. Whatever.

On we go to reciting *The Night before Christmas* at Mother's family church on a late December evening after practicing on and off with her for weeks beforehand until I had memorized it perfectly, usually when I got home from school where I was in second grade, and I remember it was my first big lesson about the relationship between my own work and reward, and from all the attention I got afterward, including what I thought was her novel approval of me, another lesson as well in the form of a dim realization that virtue might offer more in recompense than just itself.

That's one recollection this poem brings to mind but before that, even before kindergarten, I remember *The Little Engine that Could*, the story of how hard work, persistence, and confidence in yourself will get you over the top, no matter how steep the grade—another one of Mother's all-time favorites although not much footage in there about what happens once you do make the grade—and even if you don't make it the first time how important it is always to keep trying until you do, which you will, sooner or later.

But this is a poem about the second half of the train ride, after you've reached the top, when you think, "I thought I could," when you start down the other side and gravity begins to exert its power on you and the rolling stock you are coupled to and the thousands of tons of whatever it is you've been pulling is now pushing you and you realize this is more than you bargained for and unless you can slow the thing down, somewhere along the line you will end up not making a curve and everything will come off of the rails and a heap of scrap metal will be all that is left.

Brakes.

Of course, that is the answer and any son of a railroad man knows the answer has taken three different forms: first there were brakes on each car adjusted by hand by a brakeman riding the train, often having to jump from car to car to do what was needed—not a job for the faint-hearted, after which, over a hundred years ago, George Westinghouse had the idea of using compressed air in a system connecting all the train's brakes which could be controlled entirely by the engineer from the cab, and during the Age of Steam that was what everyone used until the diesel locomotive came along.

And that's when, I recently learned, we got dynamic braking, a very clever idea, which uses the force of gravity pulling on the weight of the train and turning its wheels to actually slow itself down. A diesel locomotive uses a diesel engine to produce electricity to run traction motors to turn its wheels—which is how it works going uphill, but when you are coming down if you disconnect the motors from the engine you can hook up a system in which the wheels are turning the motors rather than the motors turning the wheels, in effect, taking some of the force of gravity from the wheels and converting it to electricity—the motors exerting torque that is opposite from the rolling direction which slows down the train in the process.

The electricity can be used, or, with a bank of onboard resistors, dumped in the form of heat, lots of heat, but heat that can be gotten rid of with the help of giant fans blowing the heated air away from the locomotive, fans which make a distinctive sound you could call a whine but if you wanted to be more precise, you could say was more like the sound from an incredibly powerful invisible cello endlessly playing a note like middle C, which is how it sounded not that long ago when my father and I were up in the vineyard and the stone-train from Leheigh heading to Baltimore went by far down in the valley.

"Hear the dynamic brakes?" he asked, and I had to admit not only didn't I know what sound he was talking about but even what he was talking about until he explained it to me and after I marveled a bit at the ingenuity of it all, and remembered some pretty wild rides I had had of my own where I could have used something like this, he said—almost offhandedly— "Yes, using the forward motion of the train to brake the train is a smart idea—it's the train braking itself—but you have to get used to the noise."

Energy Lesson

$E = mc^2$
Einstein's Equation was
a formula known by
Wernher von Braun—

incontrovertibly
smart—it's a wonder no
Nazi nukes ever land-
ed on London.

Foolery

Valerie Plame was a covert intelligence agent
Whose work never drew public comment,
But when her diplomat husband said, "No,
Bush's stories simply aren't so,"
Bush men outed her ass the next moment.

When things started going bad in Iraq,
And prewar intelligence was taking a knock,
Libby called the *Times'* Miller for help,
She jumped right away when he yelped,
Earning again the sobriquet, Miss Run Amok.

George Tenant was a company man
With juicy tidbits on Iraq and Iran,
He gave Bush what he wanted
And never seemed daunted,
Got the Medal of Freedom, then ran.

Wolfowitz's advice to the President stank
And his policies on war were unfailingly rank,
But when things came apart
Bush awarded the fart
Top job at the rich and prestigious World Bank.

When Bush is fighting an implacable foe
And wishing the law allowed him further to go,
It's Alberto he calls,
Whose tomes out he hauls,
Finding exactly the cite he needs pronto.

Cheney, Rumsfeld, Powell and Rice played their part,
Now the light at end of the tunnel's quite dark,
Bush has to play his last card,
The times they are hard,
Thanks to the Three Musketeers plus Joan of Arc.

February 2, 2007

Four Boats

A large oil painting
hangs in my study
over a piano
once belonging to
my father-in-law,
a piano now mostly used
to carry family photographs.
The painting used to hang in
Charleston, South Carolina
in the window of a shop
on Calhoun Street;
I studied it on walks
when I was working there.

There are four boats in a scene
of mostly sky and water—
the waves like those in the seascapes
of Dutch painting hundreds of years ago—
and a ribbon of hills along the coast
nestling a town of low buildings
on the shore.

The centerpiece is
a warship headed south,
square rigged,
no spanker,
but every other inch of canvas flying;
there is a sloop-rigged yacht of old design
on a reach headed west;

a fishing boat with
fore and aft sails full,
beating north;
a small boat,
barely visible,
gaff rigged,
under bare poles,
headed southeasterly.

The idea of four boats,
all different,
all going in different directions
on the same northwest wind
must have been a challenge,
but the artist brought it off
so well that at first
you didn't even notice.
I think that was why I bought it.

Geraniums

Once,
several years ago,
 I wrote a poem with the opening lines:

"Death is like the shadow of geraniums
blooming by the window
bathed in winter light."

Not bad, I think,
imagery good,
nice alliteration; rhythm ok.

But today,
being here together,
I feel it's worth noting

we, you and I,
are not the shadows,
or even close to being the winter light.

And we are certainly not the window,
and anyone can tell
we're far from being the pot

the geraniums are planted in—
though it's possible someday
we may be the dirt in it.

No,
today we are
the geraniums.

Getting Dark

Late,
outside,
on cloudless summer days,
he liked to watch
the blue-painted sky,
like a perfect wash
on watercolor paper,
gradually give up its light.
From the moment
Venus first appeared
in the southwestern sky
until the night closed in completely,
he could almost feel the turning earth;
"And yet it moves," he thought,
like Galileo.

Unlike the morning when
Thus Spake Zarathustra often fit his mood,
now it was the third of the *Four Last Songs* of Strauss
his eyes invited him to hear once more
when he went inside to sleep.

Havre de Grace

is
the voice that answers,
love coming to meet,
finding a response,
waiting a return,
where the river
meets the sea
and drowns,
all, and all
there
is.

Hope

Past,
imperfect;
present,
tense.
Soon,
past
tense,
future,
perfect.

Hopper

Through the curved glass
in the middle of the painting—
the only one of his to show the glass itself—
a solitary man in a dark suit and grey fedora
is sitting at the wedge-shaped restaurant bar
with a cup of coffee,
his back facing us,
perhaps looking at the couple across from him,
perhaps not,

the couple also with their coffee,
the man in a dark suit and tie,
a dark blue shirt and also a grey fedora,
arm resting on the bar,
a cigarette between the fingers of his hand,
the other hand out of sight,
his gaze intent on something out in front of him,
perhaps the man behind the counter
whose gaze seems intent on him,
perhaps not;
all men you'd guess with no illusions;

and the woman next to the second man,
the elbow of one arm propped on the bar,
her hand holding a book of matches
which she is looking at,
perhaps thinking it's not as easy as it should be,
like striking a match is easy,
or perhaps thinking that it is,
her other arm resting on the bar,
extended toward the man,

their two hands almost touching
but not quite,
and everyone in silence.

Two large stainless coffee urns,
and a closed, narrow kitchen door
with a small window —
also dark,
the usual sugar, salt, and pepper shakers,
napkin holders, and an empty glass
complete the scene,
and the light,
the only light,
is coming from inside the bar,
a light which illuminates everything inside,
a deserted sidewalk just outside the restaurant,
and a row of cropped, brick building fronts
across the empty street.

The way the light falls on the man and woman,
the bar, the man behind the bar,
the urns, the other lone customer,
and reflects from the empty barstools,
you'd have to say the light is coming from above;
all the light is coming from above,
and also from inside.

Intelligent Design

Creation never. . .comes to the end of its design.
Harold Arlen

All of life, examined carefully,
the coiners of this term believe,
reveals a creative intelligence
on a transcendental scale.

Yes, it is a bit too anthro-
pomorphic for my taste,
but I can work with this idea of God,
even though, like the Epicureans, I wonder
when I see the world around me
whether God can be both
all powerful and all good.

To be honest,
when I hear the word "design"
the next word that comes to mind is "build."
Design is how a house is planned,
and "intelligent" means
you can get to the dining room
from the kitchen
without going through the bedroom
or the bath.

Sometimes design,
even intelligent design,
can seem a little strange.
When my grandmother died,
my grandfather moved a day-bed
to his kitchen to save going up

two flights to his bedroom
when he wished to take a nap.
But it wasn't long before he spent
his nights down there as well;
creating a design not often seen,
but nonetheless, intelligent.

In the grand debate of Darwin v. Intelligent Design,
regardless of the side you're on,
I've noticed no one argues whether
change is part of creation
just like life and matter.
One of Newton's Laws might say
things keep going on as they are
unless something alters them,
but what the footnote says is
something always does.
Change is part of life,
that much seems agreed.
So what's all the fuss about?

Regarding how life changes,
what Darwin argued has two parts:
species evolve through mutation
and natural selection —
as long as they keep reproducing and competing.

The desire for sex and power hasn't failed us yet,
so the problem with his theory can't be this proviso
(although in Darwin's explanation of our origins
these instincts are so essential, I can see
how those with concepts of the Creator
more circumspect than mine might take offense.)

Natural selection—
the success of hereditary traits
better suited to their environment—
hardly seems debatable,
so the problem must be with mutation:
the idea of a sudden, fundamental change in genes,
transferable to generations yet-to-come.

To make sure creation never comes
to the end of its design,
God could have chosen this approach,
so in and of itself, mutation's not the problem either.
Perhaps the problem with mutation is with us.
We love the charm of chance,
like winning the lottery
or the jackpot in Las Vegas,
but we hate its unpredictability.
Hearing nature doesn't have a plan
troubles our teleologic sense.
When a good or bad thing happens
we want to think there's a reason for it.
Even a mind as great as Einstein's
had trouble accepting chance
as part of creation.
"God does not play dice," he said.
Still and all, mutation is a fact of life,
and we can't rule out the possibility
God understands Vegas
even if we don't.

Life does go on
as it did for our ancestors
and as it did without the Dodo bird,
Tyrannosaurus Rex, and the Neanderthals.

It will go on without us too—
and our kind as well,
if it should come to that,
suggesting mutation and natural selection
are intelligent design
even if we aren't.

Journey Home

Beginning

There, at the station
where his cousin dropped him,
alone, surrounded by cold concrete and steel,
a place deserted at this time of day,
you see him pay his fare,
pass through the turnstile,
then ride up the escalator
to the elevated station platform,
like a bubble in water
rising smoothly to the surface.

On the platform,
he steps through the open door of a waiting car,
empty, except for two fellow-passengers
seated apart from each other.
He takes a place
at a distance from them both,
and after a bell signals the closing of the doors,
the train begins to move,
descending with increasing speed
toward its first stop en route to the city.

On one side, cars rush by on a super highway
and disappear to the rear
while those on the other side,
appear to speed up when he slows down,
and then disappear ahead of him.
The train car window
frames block after block of small rowhouses,

set back along the grid of narrow streets,
the streets deserted, except for cars;
he sees a shopping mall, a steeple pointing to the sky.

 A recorded voice names each upcoming station.
The train slows then stops
and a few passengers get off or on.
Then the train moves on again,
toward the next station
where the process is repeated,
each passenger carrying out a plan,
unmindful of the others,
all the uncoordinated plans
putting them on the train together.

After several stops,
the train disappears underground.
Outside, the tunnel lights fly by between the stations.
Inside, he opens the newspaper to his favorite page,
takes out his pen, reads the clues,
fills in the empty boxes.
Then it's time for him to leave this train for another.
He takes the escalator from the platform
to the vast underground room on the floor above
furnished with kiosks, fare machines, and turnstiles.

Next, it's up the escalator
to the cavernous hall of stone
and classic architecture
filled with throngs of people
and the giant screen of arrivals and departures.

Middle

He finds the gate and train he's looking for
and lucky for him, the train is boarding
so he doesn't have to wait like many others
killing time on the station's wooden benches.
Just time to buy a coffee and a pastry for the trip
before heading down the stairs with the others
to where the big train prepares to leave.

He thought this would be the best part of the trip,
the real train, not the dowdy metro buses
and commuter subway trains at either end,
but a train with an engineer, tickets
and a conductor to punch them,
a snack car, reclining seats and restrooms;
and best of all, speed,
the world flying by at one hundred miles an hour,
sometimes even faster
when the distance between stops
was great enough to really open up the throttle.

So he took a window seat and waited.
A train leaving on the track next to him
made him think the trip had begun
but when he looked across the aisle,
confused at first by being motionless,
he realized he hadn't moved at all
and was still waiting for the trip to start.

And when it did start, a few minutes later,
he was surprised to find he was riding backwards,
looking back on where he'd been
rather than where he was going.

His first instinct was to change his seat
but soon they were in the tunnel under the city,
and with only featureless darkness outside, let it pass.

When they emerged into the light,
he became accustomed to the sense that the city,
the older suburbs racing by,
the open country of settled farms and country roads
were all rapidly dwindling in the distance;
that the things he enjoyed looking at
always moved away from him.

Sooner than he wished,
the train began to reach
the outer limits of the city where he lived,
the home he was returning to
and the last leg of his journey.
He gathered up his few possessions
and prepared to disembark.

Unlike all the other stops along the way
this one was the last
and everyone on board was getting off.
Some got up, took their bags down,
and waited in the aisle
even though the train was moving.
Some, like him, were in no hurry
and lingered in their seats until the train had stopped.

End

He caught a bus,
a newer model with some rear-facing seats,
and he took one of those.

A man, traveling with his wife and two sons,
ages twelve and nine it turned out,
took the seat next to him,
and for a while they rode in silence.

He thought he might enjoy the ride home more
if they talked
and so he asked where he was from
and learned that it was Mexico
and they were on a holiday.
Such an easy conversation ensued
that he only noticed once or twice
the usual landmarks of his trip home
receding in the distance.

He gave him some tips on where to start their tour
and what to see while they were there,
where to do the shopping
his wife was looking forward to,
and places they might eat.
When he got off at the stop nearest his house
he knew he had made a friend
even though a fleeting one.

And now the last block:
past a modest restaurant
where he sometimes ate with friends,
past the school where a giant black and friendly man
led grade-school kids in their daily exercises,
past the cherry trees in Easter bloom
opposite the steepled church,
past the café where he had his morning coffee,
and then the turn up the street to his house.

When he unlocked the door and opened it,
all the joy of being home flooded over him:
seeing his books, his chair, the kitchen table,
all the things they'd owned so many years
and moved so many times;
later, when she came home,
holding her in his arms.
It had been quite a day.

Here was joy free of desire, a full heart;
here was unhurried time
like spring water flowing gently to the stream;
here was the easy comfort of familiar surroundings,
here was the connection to the past and tomorrow,
here was seeing one you love
coming in the distance.

Here was Hemingway's *good place,*
Dvorak's *New World,*
Copland's *Appalachian Spring,*
Dante's *Paradise.*
Here was the exaltation
of coming home to all he loved —
like a lifelong journey
covered in a day.

Karma

There's
trying harder
staying the course
playing to win
going for broke

seeing red
keeping your cool
getting even
betting the farm
going for the gold

taking your comfort
having your way
throwing them out
showing no mercy
killing with kindness;

there's
this far and no further
fight to the finish
wait till next year
show them who's boss;

there's even
thinking things through
doing what's right
and putting first things
where they should be.

All such grasping
to please
our self
is karma
it's true;

I want to get
beyond karma,
but wanting that—
just for me—
is karma too.

Life

In a universe
of countless stars
and trackless space
too vast
to comprehend,
how rare,
how wonderful,
how mysterious,
amidst
the rock,
the gas,
the primal forces,
life's earthly
appearance is—
rarer still,
human life,
and,
more recent.
The mystery
of its meaning
will only
deepen
and reasoned
conclusions
multiply
when we
come to know
there is life
in other worlds,

on other
distant Earths
orbiting
other distant stars,
some,
much like our own.

Light

J.M.W. Turner Exhibition
National Gallery of Art
October 1, 2007 – January 6, 2008

In many of the paintings,
you face the light,
not what the light
is falling on,
but the light itself.
You face it squarely.
Standing before
The Burning of the Houses
  of Lords and Commons,
or in front of
Ulysses Deriding Polyphemus,
or *Nordham Castle, Sunrise,*
you face the light,
a fire
at first destroying,
next offering hope,
then granting peace;
each fire
transcendent,
inscrutable,
humbling,
like looking into
the eye of God.

Lines

Whenever I am asked
what most I like about the beach
I always say, "The line."
Of course it really isn't there at all —
what looks like a line is only the great sea
with the great sky behind it,
the horizon an apparent, but unreal junction,
of the two.

But real lines do exist
famous boundary lines like Mason-Dixon
and not so famous ones
like those that separate my lot from my neighbor's;
the short, straight one in Euclidean geometry;
humble lines like water, sewer, gas,
electric and phone;
people lines of all kinds — mostly waiting —
like theatre or receiving;
but chorus lines are different;
so are singer's lines
and actor's lines;
there's the Maiginot Line,
the Thin Red Line,
battle lines,
the line in the sand,
the lines we dare not cross
and those we're dared to cross and do;
lines dropped to a friend
or fed to girls on dates,
(sometimes to total strangers),
product lines and fashion lines,

even lines of poetry
like Wordsworth wrote above Tintern Abbey;
and dangerous lines:
a line of cocaine,
or the flat one on the monitor above the bed—
the end of the line.

Lost World 2001

I hear a certain sadness
in the waltzes of Strauss,
a note of something loved
passing,
or almost over,
or perhaps already gone;

maybe what a woman feels
after a birth,
or when her child's innocence
dies away.

I think Stanley Kubrick heard it too.
Why else would he pair
the Blue Danube Waltz
with an earth-orbiting satellite
and its human cargo,
in a shot of the planet
from fathomless space?

More Foolery

When McCain picked running mate Palin,
his aides thought John must be failin'—
Turn down a bridge to nowhere?
Give Alaskan wildlife a scare?
How could *she* help get their man in?

Sarah Palin governed Alaska,
but longed to move up the ladder—
as a hockey-mom ex-beauty Queen,
and pro-lifers to whom she was keen—
for McCain it was easy to ask her.

John and Sarah both favor more drilling,
offshore, onshore, for sure, they are willing
to drill no matter the cost,
for oil whatever is lost—
an energy program most chilling.

Sarah's sister wed a State trooper
but decided her choice was a blooper
when he Tasered her son,
broke the law with her gun
which he grabbed, then shot a moose for her.

Sarah Palin likes burgers of moose,
and giving her foes a sharp goose,
Cheney was bad
and that made us mad,
but imagine this gal VP on the loose.

Sarah's stolen the scene from Obama
giving John hope for a new futurama,
the media's off to do vetting,
on dreams they'll be wetting,
when done with this soap opera drama.

August 30, 2008

North Rim

I am sitting at my usual table
below the Grand Canyon's North Rim,
a photograph according to the inscription,
made by Ansel Adams,
part of The Mural Project, 1941-1942.

Here I am drinking my coffee,
watching the morning patrons come and go,
ordering their eggs and bacon, or bagels,
or the special which happens to be French Toast—
wondering about the day Adams made the picture
of this vast, silent landscape,
what he had for breakfast,
what he was thinking that day setting up his camera
as the world stood on the rim of devastation
that would become the Second World War.

Did he reflect on other fragments
of the world he'd photographed?
Did he juxtapose the endless work for peace
with the endless fact of war?
And if so, did he take comfort in his art?
Or did he simply pray that day
to find the light he needed?

Not that it matters what he thought.
The world goes on as it always has
just like the unseen river in his picture,
still winding its way between the canyon walls,
cutting deeper, still creating one landscape,
still destroying another.

Now

Living in the moment
is a spiritual exercise
reminiscent of what we said
in graduate school
about the PhD program:
a process of learning
more and more
about less and less
until we know
everything
there is to know about
nothing.
Living in the moment—
now,
is like that:
finding an ever smaller
quantity of time
being neither past
nor future
in which happens
everything we do
and then becomes
everything we are—
up to now,
and everything we become—
afterwards.
All.
Nothing.

Obama

There he is
in front of an amazing crowd,
a crowd like one
from an old *Where's Waldo?*.

The shot is taken from his rear
and from above
but we instantly know who it is
even without the headline.

By now, he's like a well-known brand:
the thin frame, dark suit,
the close-cropped head,
the ears, the wave.

We also know he's smiling.
He's in Berlin, it's 2008,
but it's like Lindbergh
in Paris, 1927:

the young American hero
arrives in Europe,
another ocean crossed,
another historic flight.

Old Blood and Guts

was what they called him;
and his story,
as recounted by the movie,
confirms the label's well-deserved.
War was what he loved
and the battlefield was
where he always longed to be.

In a little scene,
often overlooked,
just before the famous slap,
we see Patton talking with the wounded,
bonding with his men,
sharing as best he could,
in their suffering,
in their sorrow.

It might mean something to you,
we hear him say up there on the screen,
dominating everyone around him,
the last German I saw didn't have a chest;
he didn't have a head either
for that matter.

The boy he says this to
just smiles a little
but doesn't speak.
You can't tell what he's thinking,
whether he agrees the three star's tidbit
is a comfort,
or it isn't;

whether he wants to say,
God have mercy on his soul
and his family,
but thinks better of it;
or perhaps he's recalling
what he and his GI buddies
often said about the man
with a pearl-handled pistol on his hip
and a helmet on his head—
this great American warrior—
our blood, his guts.

Pairs

For years now,
I almost always start the day with a poem
courtesy of Garrison Keillor
on The Writer's Almanac.

Right after the poem come
the birthdays, mostly of writers
who share the same date,
and a rendering of their work and lives.

On the last two days though,
we've had a poem from a pair of poets,
yesterday Mark Strand and Jim Harrison,
today, Vijay Seshadri and Robert Bly.

I don't recall Keillor doing this before,
and I'm not sure I like it much —
after all, a pair of poets isn't like a pair of socks,
a pair of pants, or even a pair of jacks.

But I'm willing to admit
it's a format that might go well
with the birthday combinations of those
who seem to have so little in common.

So far in May,
for example,
on four different days
we've had Irving Berlin and Salvadore Dali,

Robert Browning and Eva Peron,
Orson Welles and Randall Jarrell,
Soren Kierkegaard and Karl Marx,
to mention just a few unlikely pairs

who've turned up recently together,
if not at the same party,
at least on the same page.
Imagine, on those same days, a pair of poems

from Mary Oliver and Charles Bukowski,
Charles Simic and Maya Angelou,
Sharon Olds and Hayden Carruth,
Billy Collins and Galway Kinnell.

Peripheral Vision

I'm told the eye for reading
is not the same
as the eye for seeing:

the eye that finds a familiar shape
in a passing cloud
differs from

the eye that takes in
not only that single cloud
but all the other clouds

and the unvarying sky behind them
in every direction. I agree
there are different eyes

and much might be made of
the difference —
the value of one versus the other,

the metaphors, the analogies,
the deeper meanings
comparing them might suggest.

But I also see in both that edge
where every image vanishes —
the limit of the eye,

the very edge of vision
we cannot see beyond
with either eye.

Power House

It's a building for elegant offices now,
a model of recycled urban industrial architecture,
brimming with conference rooms and oriental carpets
where workers generate presentations in PowerPoint
instead of electric power from steam-driven turbines
for noisy streetcars that once crisscrossed the city.

Next door,
what was once a flour mill now is condominiums,
but like the streetcars, the old rendering plant is gone
as is the ash house that was further down the river,
replaced with trendy mixed-use developments above
and convenient underground parking below.

Still standing though,
atop the brick and glass Power House,
like a giant vase from a bygone era,
is a smokestack rising defiantly to the sky,
a memento of the time
when things were—well, simpler.

Of course there's no smoke coming from the stack
now, in these days of global warming;
it's as green today as a rainforest,
as quiescent as an extinct volcano;
nothing but cell phone signals being emitted
from a band of transmitters halfway up its length.

Which appears to be its only real use—
which is something anyway—
better than nothing, most would say.

Unless of course, you think the couple
sitting at the next table talking on their cell phones
would be better off talking to each other.

Unless, of course, they are.

QED

Stands for
Quod erat demonstrandum,
and translated, means
That which was to be demonstrated,
a sort of *Amen* for math proofs.

The Greeks used it—
such greats as Euclid
and later Archimedes;
it became popular again
with math types
in the European Renaissance
and was even picked up
by philosophers then,
most notably,
Spinoza.

The question is:
why not by poets
of that age?
Wikipedia tells us
a 1604 math proof of
Flemish clergyman,
Philippe van Lansberge,
contains it—
a person and a proof
(in Latin)
I never heard of.

So I have to ask:
was his a greater truth in those times
than Shakespeare's answer of love
to the question of why,
though tired,
we go on,
or Donne's analysis of why
the bell that tolls,
tolls for us all?
Or Herrick's proposition to virgins
to make much of time,
or Marvell's determination
of when coyness is
a crime?

I don't think so.
Poets had a chance then
to show the common core
of both poetry and math
but missed it—
one explanation,
perhaps,
why today
we have both
the BS
and the MFA.

Question

"What then shall we do?"
Although Tolstoy asked it
of the rich, about the poor of Moscow
many years ago,
it's a question we often hear
today as well.

Some say, "Save yourself,"
survive as best you can.
escape the world around you;
build another world of your own inside it.

Sometimes we can,
but not for long.
"The battalions wheel!" sang Mother Courage.
And when they do
that little world is shattered.

Some choose to object:
"This far and no farther,"
like Rosa Parks,
who refused to yield her seat,
wouldn't move to where the law required.
It takes courage to object.
Some die for their objections,
sometimes gloriously
but most times not.

Some choose to take revenge,
to punish or get even;
"Make them pay!"

Faced with terror
they resort to it themselves,
other's excesses excuses for their own.

Some, like Tolstoy,
keep trying to be kind:
"Love your neighbor," is their mantra;
others, resigned to the world as it is
choose to accept things as they are.
"The poor are with you always."

"What then shall we do?"

Real Time

From simple beginnings, our universe
has evolved over 13 billion years.
Martin Rees

When it gets dark,
go outside,
look at the night sky.

Close your eyes.
Think:
I am in the present instant,
the moment,
now.

Now open your eyes.
Look at the stars.
Each bit of light you see,
the very photons now falling on your retinas,
began their existence and
started a journey toward Earth long ago:

the light from the Pleiades, 440 years ago,
from the Orion Nebula, 1,500 years ago,
from the Crab Nebula, 6,000 years ago,
from Andromeda, the galaxy nearest our own,
2 million years ago.

So in a moment of time,
you can see two million years of time.
From Hubble, you can see the light
from sources further out,
from the Sombrero Galaxy,

the now arriving light
that began and left there 25 million years ago,
and from the Spiral Galaxy, 98 million years ago,
and the galaxy cluster Abell 1689, 2 billion years ago,
from the Constellation Fornax, 13 billion years ago.

With Hubble,
in an instant of time,
you can see an instant of all time.

Rolling Thunder

Today, as is the custom here
on Memorial Day,
bikers by the thousands
motorcycle through our city
to give the missing dead in war
their due.

In an ancient poem of Horace
the voice of an unburied sailor
washed upon the shore
implores a traveler there
to pause a moment
and give three handfuls of sand
to cover up his corpse.
The voice reminds him
he may need the rites someday
and may be disdained if he refuses:
"I will not unavenged unburied be,"
he says.

I like to think today is all a reenactment
of the scene imagined by the poet
two thousand years ago;
every biker—a traveler,
the missing—the sailor,
Rolling Thunder—three handfuls of sand.

Soul Music

When I heard the Queen of Soul
singing in an outdoor plaza
by a manmade lake,

belting out the tune
and spelling out the lyrics
of R-E-S-P-E-C-T,

and before that heard Brother Ray
sing some soul from a bandstand
in Rock Creek Park,

and then years later heard Stevie Wonder
sing the Our Father, a cappella,
while sitting in our church

for a little boy who'd died
while we, sitting there with him,
like Jesus, wept,

I knew soul is not the music of the spheres
but the music of our breathing,
of our consciousness;

the music of our hearts breaking,
of being lost and found,
of falling hard,

the music of our getting up,
looking back,
and sometimes turning back,

the music of our going on,
surrendering,
and starting over.

But sometimes I can't hear the music;
the voices fade,
the music seems to stop.

Then I ask, *where are the voices now?*
I listen for the music.
I need to hear again.

Space Time

In space time
there is no space
unless there is something in it,
a point of reference.
Take away life,
the world,
the universe of ponderable bodies,
and the laws of each,
then nothing would remain,
not even space,
since space is nothing
without something.
Maybe there is a problem with the verb "to be"
but if something is nothing
isn't nothing something?

Speed of Light

When someone used to have a bright idea
really good, but too different to accept,
people would say, "He's ahead of his time."

I wouldn't have given this a second thought
but this year I've been learning physics
or, I should say, trying to.

If I'm correct, the only way anyone (or anything)
can be ahead of his time is to travel faster
than the speed of light. That is,
even faster than 186,000+ miles per second,
which is itself a wicked speed.

If I could leave now and get to the moon that fast
I could see myself writing this poem
out here in the garden
when the image of me writing it
got there, just a little later.

And if I traveled even faster,
maybe I could get there before
I even wrote the poem.
Even before I made the morning coffee
or got out of bed.

No, it can't be done,
according to the Maestro.
The limiting velocity of the speed of light
"Neither can be reached nor exceeded
by any real body."

Of course, when people offered up their judgment
of what was too far-out for them
they weren't talking about real bodies
they were talking about the thoughts
real bodies have.

So I suppose the question is:
when the so-called light bulb comes on
does it project a beam
subject to the rules of physics?

When I asked a physicist
what he thought the answer was,
he said it does—
which is what
I thought he would.

Temptation's Opposite

If temptation is the encouragement to do wrong
by the promise of gain,
then what do we call the encouragement to do right
by the same means?

Temptation's opposite.

Bribe won't do;
associated as it is
with corruption.
Sugar-coating comes to mind,
like what surrounds a good medicine's bad taste.
But what's the word?
I've racked my brain
but can't come up with it.
Its practice is widespread—
religions are full of it,
at least the ones I've looked into;
so is parenting:
When your homework's done you can watch TV.

Words like incentive or motivation fail
because they're too broad,
too morally neutral or compromised.
Eve was motivated after all,
to eat Forbidden Fruit.

We do have hope—
wishing for what's right
with expectation of fulfillment
also redemption—

release from blame,
something we wouldn't need
if we'd done what's right instead;
forgiveness —
the right thing to do when wronged;
and virtue —
doing the right thing
which we're told is its own reward.

But temptation's opposite?
It's curious.
We don't seem to have
a word for it.

The Point

I speed up the hill this morning
in my electric golfcart,
up the steep farm road,
looking down each long row,
the vines dwindling in the distance.

I can see my grandfather sixty years ago
going up this same farm road,
to this same field,
walking behind two old mules
to plow five acres of foot-high corn.

Maybe the point for him up here
was clear but I find myself wondering lately,
what's the point for me?
Though once I thought I knew
and doubts were few,

now my sureness is steadily receding,
like the vines, and I see, also like the vines,
whatever the point might be
for me, it too
is vanishing.

Time

Time marches on
but suppose it didn't.
Time waits for no man
but suppose it did.
"In time's a noble mercy
of proportion"
but suppose it wasn't.
What a world —
if time didn't fly,
wasn't of the essence,
didn't heal all wounds.
What a marvel is
this time we have
when we imagine
what life would be
without it.

nobody knows
what it is — TIME
Nietzie's eternal
rebirth theory (1)

267

Toward the Distant Woods

In addition to the milk-cows,
Strawberry and Spot,
my grandfather had two old mules,
Ginny and Kate.

Year-after-year,
they pulled the plow and harrow,
mowed and raked the hay,
dragged the stone sled,
spread the cow's manure and their own,
hauled the corn to crib,
hay and fodder to the barn,
planted all the seeds.
In summer, work done,
they grazed the pasture.
They wintered in the barn,
coming out once a day
for light and water.

One spring day,
after mowing peas all morning,
Grandpa unhitched them from the mower
and let us ride them bareback to the barnyard
where they could get some rest and water.
Headed down the hill,
Grandpa leading them by their bridles,
suddenly they broke away from him
and took off running hard
through last year's cornfield,
still unplowed.

We were small then
and we didn't ride for long.
Bouncing off,
it was only luck
we weren't impaled on the stubby cornstalks
or knocked senseless by the steel-shod hooves.
But none of that happened.
The shouts behind us only made the mules run faster,
galloping at breakneck speed
toward the distant woods.

Of course they finally had to stop
and when they did,
Grandpa went to get them,
then led them back to the only life they ever had.

We never knew for sure what set them off:
our tin pails hanging from the hames
jangling with each step they took;
or maybe it was us,
their unaccustomed riders,
they objected to.

Or maybe mules have souls.
And when they wondered, *Why do mules exist?*
the answer was more than they could bear.
Desperate, they felt they must do something
and were running out of time.

Traffic

Mid-afternoon, ten days before the solstice,
70 degrees F. despite approaching winter,
a day perfectly calm.

I face the sun,
the traffic going to and fro
between me, perched on my bench,
and the river.
On the quay, joggers, walkers,
and cyclists go by;
on the river, rowers, boaters,
and ducks make their rounds;
and above the river, the gulls patrol for fish
who make their own unseen rounds
beneath the water's surface;
a few jet planes take off upriver;
a helicopter passes low overhead,
later returns;

and on the circle of bare dirt
around the tree in front of me,
sparrows, their wings vibrating wildly, dust up,
heads cocked briefly in a dozen different angles,
as if they're eying something
but can't quite make out what.
A pigeon comes by and joins the sparrows,
settles into place, slowly,
like a car losing air from its tires.

A tall, young woman pushing a stroller,
a face like Botticelli's Flora,
stops to feed the birds,
then goes on.

All afternoon,
the sun goes one way,
the river goes the other.

Triptych

I.

There are fashions in art like anything else
and there are times when artists tire
of what they're doing as well as what's been done,
and want to try their hand at something different.
In fifteenth century Holland,
the triptych as an art form had been around for years
(a hinged writing tablet consisting of three leaves
was used in ancient Rome)
and Bosch had fully mastered it
by the time he painted this one
on three large wooden panels,
the center panel almost square and larger than a man,
side panels half its size.

II.

The Garden of Earthly Delights,
like a silent film,
tells a story in three frames:
the side panels narrate the story
of the Garden before the Fall,
and the Hell and damnation that awaits us after.
But in the center panel,
instead of the usual picture
 illustrating all our sins,
Bosch paints paradise —
what those who're saved might expect,
after the Apocalypse,
when all power of evil is destroyed
and God reigns forever.

The first thing to notice is there are lots of people
(a bit of a surprise) and they all are naked,
but innocent of their nakedness,
like Adam and Eve before the Fall,
young and alike but not identical;
yes, there is some sex—
but nothing that looks like lust,
just the heart's free affection;
no anger, no envy, no greed, no sloth;
eating, yes, but no gluttony, no pride;
no human folly,
no ship of fools,
no overbearing prince or church,
no haughty aristocracy.

In a world without sin
everyone is having fun,
sometimes standing on their heads,
doing somersaults or dancing,
picking fruit and eating it,
enjoying the songs of birds,
kissing and caressing,
bathing, swimming,
riding animals in a circle like a carousel,
playing games that look like hide-and-seek,
sometimes just chasing one another;
everyone sharing the pleasure of delight.
It's like nursery school at recess,
or maybe Mardi Gras or Carnival;
updated to our time,
a vision of paradise, if we have one,
not vastly different from our own.

Everyone's grown up but very young,
children in adult bodies but children nonetheless,
the children of God,
the last men and women
at the end of time.

III.

On the front panel of his work when closed,
Bosch paints a haunting image:
a dimly lighted sphere in a darkened square,
(a small figure of God in the upper left-hand corner —
almost a parenthesis);
here is a bubble suspended in the dark,
and in the bubble a gray world,
wet and soggy,
a little dry land here and there,
and the overcast sky above,
cloudy,
with a chance of rain.

Two Windows

It's raining here this morning, a steady rain,
a cold rain you can hear falling gently on the roof,
and in the upstairs backroom study,
sitting in my leather chair
facing two tall, shuttered windows
with a large street map of our village
hanging on the wall between them,

I look out through the open louvers of one window
on a bare, coral brick wall, on nothing
but the plain American bond of my neighbor's house,
and through the other window,
on some gray sky,
a jungle of garden shrubs and trees,
and the bare branches of a tree far in the distance;

and the contrast between the two windows
is so great,
to the untutored eye,
you could believe
you were in two different places:
an office cubicle buried in a light shaft,
or a rustic cabin deep in the woods,

but I know what I am seeing is all part of one place,
one place depicted on my map
as an ordinary plot of land
surrounded by my neighbors' plots,
and on mine just another house set close to the corner
of two perpendicular, intersecting streets
and therefore close to the houses built behind it.

All so simple really,
like the toast and tea
you brought up earlier on a tray,
the warm cup held between my hands,
the cozy new roof installed last summer,
and the whole room filling slowly, generously,
with the rain-soaked morning light.

Unknown Zone

That little message appearing briefly
on the lower right hand corner of the PC screen?

Were he still around,
Dante might call it Purgatory —
the place of temporary punishment —
coming as it does between ordinary life
and connection to the WorldWideWeb,
next to either Heaven or Hell
depending on how you look at it.

And our click on the Internet Explorer icon
just before the suggestive little message appears?
That's the beginning of the modern-day Afterlife,
the moment when one door closes
and another is said to open.

Yes, the PC Unknown Zone
is a perfect metaphor for Purgatory
and may seem even more so
for those with DialUp
than those with DSL.

Utopia

This morning I was reading
Sir Thomas More's *Utopia*
and wondering why we don't hear
much about this subject any more.

We've hardly found the place
where poverty and misery
have been erased,
so that can't be the reason.

I looked up the word and found
its origin was Greek
and their meaning was "no place,"
which started me to thinking.

The modern world has come to understand
Utopia is not a state of nature
or a set of rules we play by
but a state of mind.

I guess that puts Henry David Thoreau,
the likes of Thomas Merton,
and the Dali Lama
squarely in the More tradition.

The literature on Utopia hasn't gone away
it's simply changed its focus
from the ideal state of the body politic
to the serenity of the inner self.

No Garden, no Atlantis,
no theocratic City,
just how to live a tolerable life
in an intolerable world.

I suppose the "serious writers"
have taken up where Swift left off;
with horses who behave with reason
and the Yahoos, men, who behave like beasts.

They see, as Cassius did
the fault is in our selves
and if they have any hope at all,
have more for horses than for men.

Vineyard Cycle

Budbreak

The vineyard in early spring
like a field of crosses
waits for budbreak
after pruning
when happy shoots wake up
unfolding in a trice
with all the boundless energy
of life beginning once again.

Debourrement

From the budeye
a growing tip appears
pulling behind
a leaf
spring green
edged with carmine
followed by another leaf
with opposing tendril
a serpent's tongue
testing the air
then the flower cluster
not yet opened
the inflorescence
in time
the fruit.

Bloom

An army of vines
green flags flying
new bearing canes
pushing their way into the void
not yet fully understanding
seem taken by surprise
with the sudden flowering
appearing in their midst.

Veraison

Huddled together
the clustered grapes
like high-school girls
have somehow shed
their milky green
for a bronze translucence
inviting all who pass
to taste
the miracle
of ripening fruit.

Aoutment

Now the change is mostly going on inside
an ancient chemistry of grapes takes over
making the most of what's been given
but like a seventh chord
not yet resolved.

Vendage

And so it comes to this:
the gathering of the grapes
not at all the plan
contemplated by the vines
but if the age-old questions
puzzle them
it isn't showing.
Without their crop
the vines enjoy the waning sun
much lighter now
as if
they're almost glad
it's over.

When

When is the time something is done.
We tell stories when someone dies,
what we can remember of their life
to keep their mortal spirit alive for us,
to comfort us when we mourn.
The terrible moment comes when
we call to mind the time,
when no one has any memory
of the only life we've had,
when there is no one left to comfort,
when there is nothing left
for anyone to mourn—
the time something is done.

White Dwarf

To make a white dwarf
takes a star of a certain size,
not too big and not too small.

If the star's too big when it explodes,
say like a supergiant,
when all is done
you get a neutron star,
the remains of a supernova;
if it's way too big,
you get a black hole.

If it's too small,
you get a failed star
lacking the heat for nuclear fusion,
a brown dwarf.

But a star like our sun
is just right:
in another six billion years or so,
you'll get a monstrous flaring up,
a red giant engulfing all the inner planets—
including our own—
then everything around the remnant sun
collapsing in on itself,
into a ball the size of a planet—
a white dwarf.
Surrounded by a cloud of gas
lit by radiation from the burned out star,
in ten thousand more years

that light too will fade, then disappear,
leaving just a lifeless speck of stardust,
a small reminder of what once was—
if anyone's still watching
and anyone should care.

Window

I was dozing on the sofa
in a little half-sleep,
freed of time and place,
when it hit the window
like a pair of socks, tightly rolled,
thrown against the glass.
That time, I let it go, not ready yet
to bestir myself.

The second time it happened
I got up to see what was going on.
Outside, under the window was a bird
lying on the porch,
a lady cardinal I took for dead.
Approaching for a closer look
she came to life again,
shook off the impact of her crash,
and flew away.

Strange, I thought,
guessing she mistook the window
for an opening she could fly through.
Stranger still, not long after,
it happened again,
and then again and again
throughout the afternoon.

"An omen of death," my father said,
when we talked about it later.
More like a metaphor for life
than a harbinger of death, I thought—

how many times do we mistake a window
for a passage or an opportunity
only to find out otherwise—

until the next day when I found the bird
below the window, neck broken,
this time down for good.
At first I thought Father had been right
after all. But the longer I thought,
the more I saw we both were:
alive, we fly toward a place we cannot get to
death, the glass we can't get through.

X chromosome

Is not love of something, and of something too
which is wanting in a man?
Socrates, *The Symposium*

I don't think of the X chromosome
(and the ovum's 22 others)
as something I urgently want to connect with,
something I want to attract,
to impress with my prowess and strength,
excite with my daring,
seduce with my charm,
possess with my love,
but maybe unconsciously
that's what it's about—
that lovely desire—
like a feather riding an incoming wave
unaware of the real power moving it
inexorably toward
the inevitable crash on the shore,
the long glide up the sand;
what drove Leander to swim
to Hero each night
until his nocturnal swim
ended in death for them both—
for "the reason no man knows,"
according to Shakespeare.
Well, conscious or unconscious,
maybe that X chromosome could be it.

Y chromosome

This one came from my father
whose father had given him his;

together with his gamete's 22 others
and the X from my mother and her 22,

it made me a male,
but it could have been otherwise:

my father also had gametes swimming around
with X chromosomes from his mother;

they could have combined
with my mother's gamete

containing an X chromosome
from either her Mom or her Dad;

had it happened that way,
things would be different today —

it's a she I would be
and not the he that I am.

Zygote

I.

This then is the very beginning:
a new cell,
a new individual,
either of one sex or the other,
in time,
a copy of its parents,
though not an exact one.

But is all that has preceded it
more than mere biology?
Is a zygote non-being into being?
Is non-being into being
transcendence of our selves?
Is creation
a world always in the making?
Is this love?
And what of immortality?

II.

These are hard questions,
and getting answers
is much harder than solving for x
in a simple linear equation
with only a single unknown.

That every non-constant single variable
polynomial with complex coefficients
has at least one complex root
is a Fundamental Theorem of Algebra –
an idea that is demonstrably true.

But Auden's proposition
"Love each other or perish,"
remains to be proved
as a Fundamental Theorem of Life.
Violations of his premise are common
and yet we're still here –
though some may argue
it's just a matter of time.

"Live free or die," also comes to mind,
but, like Auden's proposition,
the breadth of the claim
makes it impossible to prove.

Another is "Santa doesn't exist,"
which presents a similar problem.
We can't decisively prove
Santa doesn't exist –
not because it's a negative proposition –
but rather, like the others
there's no way to test it
in every last time and place.

All we can do is infer it
from the available facts
which means you never can tell
when new information
might prove you wrong;

another way of saying
when there is no evidence
something exists,
that fact doesn't count
as decisive evidence
it doesn't.

III.

The Greeks had many ideas
about love and the meaning of life,
but none any more provable than Auden's.
According to Plato
what we love is what we care about –
what matters most to us,
what gives meaning to our lives,
what makes us happy –
the good.

Holding on to the good forever
is what we all want,
but being mortal,
having offspring,
who in turn have offspring of their own,
each new generation seeking the good
in an unending cycle,
comes as close as we can
to everlasting possession of the good
for ourselves.

IV.

So maybe,
just maybe,
we can say generation is about immortality –
or *of* immortality as the Greeks liked to say –
and so is love:
"how the whole human comedy
keeps perpetuatin' it-self –"
is the way the Mysterious Stranger puts it
to the Dude at the end of *The Big Lebowski.*

V.

In a universe
seemingly indifferent
to human happiness,
it's worthy of note
the Dude
also abides –
the one in us all
who keeps trying to find the good,
though never sure
he'll ever make sense of it all.
I take comfort in that;
as well as in the hope
that someday
we will learn more.

Acknowledgements

When you start writing poetry at age 65, it's a challenge to know where to begin—and where to end— the acknowlegements. It's certain, however, that what follows is a very partial list.

First, nothing I can say could ever account for what this work owes to my wife, Grace, whose steadfast love, ideas, and diligence made these poems and so much else possible.

Next come the poets. Reading their poetry is an integral part of my own. Two in particular, are my steady companions: Billy Collins and Stanley Kunitz.

Dan Veatch, editor of the *Atlanta Review,* also offered me some genuine encouragement which I would like to take special note of. "This one almost made it," is how he described in a hand-written note one of the poems I sent him several years ago when everyone else was sending me polite, impersonal rejection slips in my SASE's. Although he had sent me some of those slips as well, and even though he didn't publish this latest one, his note reassured me that at least I was going in the right direction.

As I have been writing these poems I have often thought of the young and friendly Marcia Hovey, one of my college English professors of many years past, and an assignment which I wrote for her in free verse instead of in the essay form she had prescribed. "Next time, follow directions," she wrote on the paper, but gave me an A anyway. Who knows where the idea of writing poetry came from so late in life—and the thought that it might be fun to do. Maybe that was the start.

Between then and now, many others have given me encouragement for which I am deeply grateful. I especially want to mention the support I received from my good friends Judy Brown, fellow poet, and her husband, David Ward. Their help has been invaluable.

Several of the poems rely heavily and directly on the work of others. Wherever possible, I have tried to be conscientious in those cases about giving appropriate credit in the poem itself, but some deserve specific mention. The material in "Weather" comes from an obituary written by Patricia Sullivan and published in the *Washington Post* on April 17, 2008. In "Life Force," the differing concepts of "finite and infinite games" come from James P. Carse's book of the same name who defines the terms this way: "a finite game is played for the purpose of winning, an infinite game for the purpose of continuing the play." In "Rainmaker," the plot summary closely follows the one given in the playbill from the Arena Stage production of 2006. The technical description in "Dynamic Braking" relies as much on Wikipedia as on the recollection of how my father described it, although I feel confident the difference between the two is negligible. Finally, "Vineyard Cycle" is based on a description of the yearly cycle for the French hybrid baco noir wine grape in Philip M. Wagner's *A Wine-Grower's Guide*. An early pioneer in eastern U.S. winegrowing, Wagner assures us "the story of the annual cycle of a specific vine growing in a specific place is essentially the story of them all."

The photographs at the beginning of Sections I and II were bought at local shops here in Washington, DC. The bocce player is a photo originally entitled "Paris," by Claude Taylor, and "The Kiss, Brancusi, Paris" is signed DeJobleso. The photo of the boys in the snow at the beginning of Section III appeared on the front page of the *Washington Post* in January 1989. We bought a copy of the photo from the *Post* because the two boys in the picture, taken at Montrose Park in Georgetown, are our sons, Matthew and Patrick, who were age six and four at the time.

Finally, the background material on the front and back covers was taken from a paper I wrote for a NATO conference on manpower planning held in Brussels, Belgium in 1965. The paper was published in *Manpower Planning* by The English Universities Press, London, 1966.

About the Author

Worth Bateman grew up in Maryland, attended public school, and graduated from McDaniel College. He won a Woodrow Wilson fellowship and went to Harvard University where he earned a PhD in economics. He served in the Kennedy, Johnson, and Carter administrations, and directed the research program at the Urban Institute. For many years he also renovated and restored old houses, one on the National Register of Historic Places. Late in his professional career, he established a wine grape vineyard at his family's farm outside Baltimore which he continued to operate after his retirement. It was during this time he took up writing plays and poetry. Today, the vineyard is gone but the writing continues. He lives with his wife Grace in Washington, DC. They have six children and three grandchildren.